I0823087

PESTS & OTHER FRIENDS

PESTS

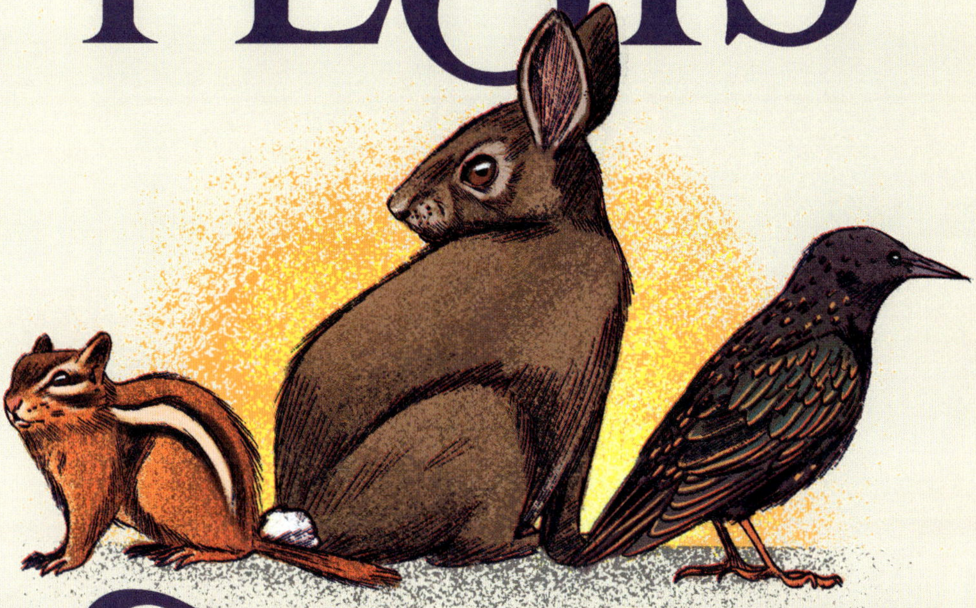

& OTHER FRIENDS

Discover the True Nature of the Most Maligned Animals

HALSEY BERRYMAN

DK

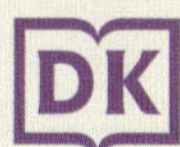

Publisher Mike Sanders
Executive Editor Alexander Rigby
Editorial Director Ann Barton
Art & Design Director William Thomas
Designer Lindsay Dobbs
Illustrator Halsey Berryman
Editorial Assistant Resham Anand
Copy Editor & Fact Checker Devon Fredericksen
Proofreaders Mira S. Park, Rose Selby
Indexer Celia McCoy

First American Edition, 2026
Published in the United States by DK Publishing
1745 Broadway, 20th Floor, New York, NY 10019

The authorized representative in the EEA is Dorling Kindersley Verlag GmbH.
Arnulfstr. 124, 80636 Munich, Germany

26 27 28 29 30 10 9 8 7 6 5 4 3 2 1
001-351406-MAR2026

Library of Congress Number: 2025942083
ISBN 979-8-2171-2813-6

Printed and bound in China

www.dk.com

This book was made with Forest Stewardship Council™ certified paper – one small step in DK's commitment to a sustainable future.
Learn more at
www.dk.com/uk/information/sustainability

For my mom, who put a pencil in my hand and empathy for animals in my heart. Her art was my first inspiration.

For Hamilton, whose favorite perch was a human head.

And for every maligned creature on Earth. May we learn to be kind to them and each other.

CONTENTS

NORTH

UBIQUITIOUS PESTS

The word "pest" originates from the Black Death, borrowed from the French *peste* and derived from the Latin root *pestis*, meaning plague. Centuries later, the term evolved to include animals who interfere with agriculture. The comparison of certain animals to disease propagates a synthetic but definitive separation between ourselves and nature. Not surprisingly, the unintended consequences of humankind's exercise of dominion over the environment has created problems for humans and animals alike. Despite the ingenuity and kindness of which humans are infinitely capable, we have fractured our relationship with nature as time has progressed, much in the way children grow up to lose their natural affinity for animals.

Over millennia, we have learned to perceive wild animals solely as impediments to human progress, losing our sense of them as partners, co-inhabitants, and fellow citizens of Earth whose presence is critical to maintaining ecological balance for all of us. Humanity has curated the world to fit its needs exclusively, a fool's errand on which it has embarked to its own detriment, on a planet where the needs of all species are inextricably linked. Human development and climate change destroy animals' natural habitats, forcing them to adapt to increasingly artificial environments. In putting our proverbial thumbs on the scale, humans have shifted the critical balance between predator and prey. So-called "pests" sometimes even thrive because of us—yet we somehow find it acceptable to stigmatize them, anyway.

As modernization and technology make our lives ever more convenient, human progress only seems to increase the number of animals we condemn. Pest status was once reserved for those who feed on crops meant for humans. Today, we slander all kinds of animals we deem inconvenient; they're road hazards, vectors of disease, garden thieves, and landscape destroyers. We sometimes resent certain animals simply because we don't find them aesthetically appealing. We malign animals of all stripes for simply daring to exist in proximity to us, and for acting in accordance with their natural instincts. We attempt to police nature as we police ourselves, and expect nature to obey, failing time and time again to confront the limits of our influence.

Virtually all animals have felt humanity's impact, yet pests are the least likely to garner our sympathy. The extinction of the white rhino draws widespread media attention, yet the plight of the pigeon, one of the most threatened bird families in the world, is casually overlooked. Because we control and monitor our exposure to animals so meticulously, our alienation from them is pervasive. Our limited interaction with them often manifests itself in conflict, and thus, our understanding of animals is rife with anthropomorphism, misinformation, and superstition. This is even built into how we talk to and about each other, commonly using derogatory stereotypes about pests to describe people, referring to the corrupt as "weasels," the cunning as "sly as foxes," and disingenuous confidants as "rats" or "moles." This reinforces these animals' bad reputations, gives us permission to villainize them, and allows us to ignore their many benefits despite the inconveniences they may cause. Maybe, as is the case with many so-called pests, the problem is humanity's expectation to keep nature separate from us, a misguided notion that mythologizes problem animals everywhere.

The animals we consider pests are derided for countless reasons. Some are considered crop pests, though we have destroyed many of their natural habitats and forced them to adapt to environments designed solely with humanity in mind. Others are considered dangerous, even though they are simply living in proximity to us and have adapted to defend themselves against predators. We even deride some animals for being invasive species, even though, in some cases, humans purposefully introduced them. Many animals are condemned simply for being abundant, which usually occurs because of human activity. Some are even the subject of cultural myths, superstitions, and misinformation, though they cause very little, if any, harm. More often than not, if an animal is considered a pest, we have made it so, one way or another.

While this book focuses on North America, pests and nuisance animals are the subject of stigma all over the world. Their status as such, whether legal or cultural, depends largely on where they live, how developed their territory is, and which industries operate there. People who live in cities have completely different relationships with pests than those who live in rural areas. A New Yorker may not view wolves as pests, whereas the rural farmers and purveyors of livestock could easily identify them, for example. Throughout this book, so-called pests are divided into regions where they are the most disparaged by their human neighbors.

All animals have conflict with other animals—that is the nature of the predator-prey dynamic. However, pests are a uniquely human invention, and nature is inherently perfect. This book helps to illuminate the truth about so-called pests, which often defies their reputations. Each has a right to live, plays a critical role in their ecosystem, and some even make our lives easier. When considering our relationship with animals, it's important to ask why some are loathed and some are loved, and if humans should feel entitled to judge them at all. Considering our role as stewards of the environment, empathy for some of the most maligned animals can help us reshape our relationship with nature, one another, and ourselves.

Hudson Bay

Appalachian Mountains

Atlantic Ocean

Gulf of Mexico

From the Megalopoli

Nort

to the Great Lakes

OPOSSUMS

Didelphis virginiana

The Virginia opossum is one of North America's most valuable and misunderstood mammals. They are despised not only for what some deem an ugly and ferocious appearance, but also for the gross misconception that they are aggressive, dirty, disease-ridden vermin that humans should fear. Their sharp teeth, fleshy hands, and spindly, prehensile tail may elicit fear and disgust in some, but they're far more scared of us than we are of them, and they provide innumerable benefits to the ecosystem and human life. While they prefer temperate, forested habitats close to a water source, opossums have expanded their range north due to climate change and adapted to life near humans, since we provide greater access to food.

Rather than biting, opossums typically ward off predators by hissing, displaying their fifty-tooth grin (more teeth than any North American mammal) or "playing dead," as they lie prone, drool, slow their heart rate, and emit an odor that imitates decay. Not only are defenseless opossums virtually harmless to humans; they also prevent the spread of disease. They can eliminate up to 90 percent of ticks that attach to them through grooming, which in turn plays a role in reducing the number of ticks likely to spread Lyme disease. Their low body temperature makes it nearly impossible for them to contract rabies, and they are resistant to most snake venom. Like many so-called pests, opossums eat carrion, which can otherwise be breeding grounds for bacteria and parasites that are harmful to humans. They love to eat roaches and crickets, and gardeners might appreciate their omnivorous diet that includes a variety of typical garden pests, as well as rotten fruit. As North America's only native marsupial, we should learn to appreciate the Virginia opossum's gentle, helpful nature rather than demonize them according to our standards of cuteness, beauty, or usefulness.

Grackles are small, iridescent blackbirds known for their signature call that resembles the sound of a loud, rusty metal gate. With an estimated population of over 70 million, large flocks of them (unaffectionately called "plagues") are a common sight. Despite their diminutive size, they can cause damage to human infrastructure. Grackles are known to roost in groups of around 3,000 or more individuals and large flocks perched on power lines can spark costly outages when they alight en masse, causing lines to collide and sway violently. As opportunistic foragers, grackles will eat almost anything, including garbage. However, during migration, they favor crop seeds and seedlings. These gregarious birds are responsible for millions of dollars of damage to corn crops every year, but they also feast on watermelon, sunflower, and peanut crops. They're even known to follow farm equipment in pursuit of their next meal. Despite the problems they cause, grackles promote biodiversity through seed dispersal and help control the populations of other crop pests like grubs, caterpillars, and beetles.

During the 18th and 19th centuries, deforestation for agriculture created a boom in grackle populations because of the increased availability of their preferred habitat and access to food. Despite being one of the most successful bird species in North America today, their population has decreased by 50 percent over the last 50 years—linked by experts to pesticides, culling, and climate change. Their numbers rise and fall dramatically because of us, yet we still dare to vilify them. Perhaps we should ask ourselves why certain animals are considered pests and who is ultimately to blame for this disparagement. Grackles are intelligent and social birds who deserve our respect.

GRACKLES

Quiscalus quiscula

STAR-NOSED MOLES

Condylura cristata

Their unusual noses contain around 100,000 nerve endings—almost six times more than human hands—giving them the best sense of touch of any mammal.

Star-nosed moles are small mammals most closely related to shrews and hedgehogs, who spend most of their lives underground. Because they are tiny, solitary, and nocturnal, they can be elusive, but they're surprisingly abundant in the United States and Canada. A telltale sign that a star-nosed mole is nearby is their trademark mounds of dirt (molehills) amidst grasses and gardens. As insectivores that prefer moist soil, these moles spend their lives digging underground in search of earthworms and insect larvae in areas close to water. Since their range coincides with some of the most populous areas in North America, they tend to clash with humans by inadvertently uprooting garden plants as their powerful claws dig tunnels just beneath the surface of the ground in search of insects. In addition to underground damage, molehills can also wreak havoc on mowers and other equipment. As unpleasant as it may be to wake up to damage caused by moles in the night, their benefits to the ecosystem and our gardens far outweigh the destruction they can cause.

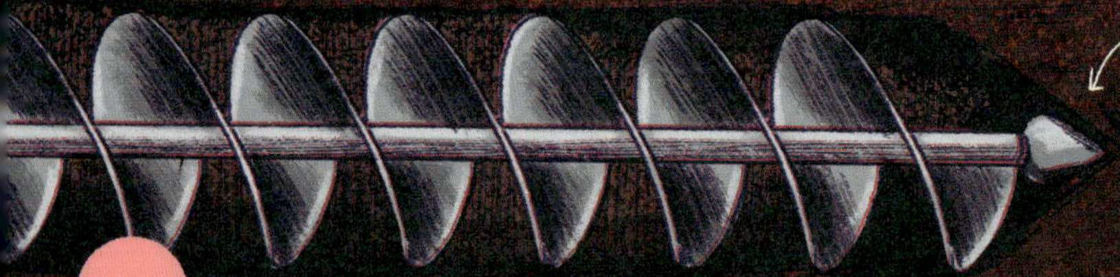

Star-nosed moles can dig up to 8 feet (2.4 m) per hour—impressive considering their average size is around 7 inches (19 cm) long and they weigh about as much as a 9-volt battery.

Star-nosed moles aerate and mix the soil, which increases soil health, and they eat the most destructive garden pests while they are still in larval form. These moles also help sustain ecosystems with heightened human activity by serving as easy prey for animals like foxes, owls, and other predators. The star-nosed mole is semiaquatic and has an excellent sense of smell and touch despite their poor eyesight. They can even smell underwater. The 22 tendrils radiating from the nostrils they're named for are covered in highly specialized sensors that help them "see" their surroundings with great precision. These unique creatures may cause some damage, but when we see molehills, we would do well to not make mountains of them and instead appreciate star-nosed moles for what they do for our gardens and the environment.

BOX TURTLES

Terrapene carolina

Often described as salmonella-ridden "speedbumps," Eastern box turtles are the deliberate target of many. According to an experiment done at Clemson University, 2 percent of all box turtles are killed intentionally by drivers, and a staggering third of respondents admitted to this cruel behavior. Box turtles aren't more prone to spreading disease than other wildlife, and people are far less likely to contract salmonella from a wild box turtle than a captive one. Since they only tend to cross roads in search of food or a place to lay their eggs, it's critical they reach their destination unharmed, as threats like the pet trade, habitat loss, and climate change continue to decimate their populations. When we see a box turtle on the road, we should help this gentle homebody by assisting its safe crossing.

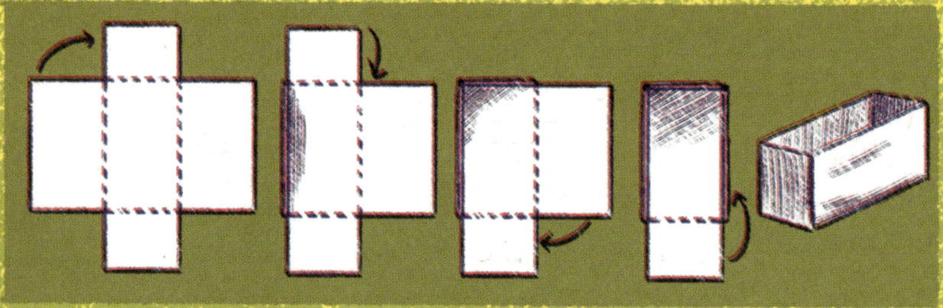

Box turtles are named after their ability to completely close their shells to protect against predators.

They spend their whole lives within 750 feet of where they were born.

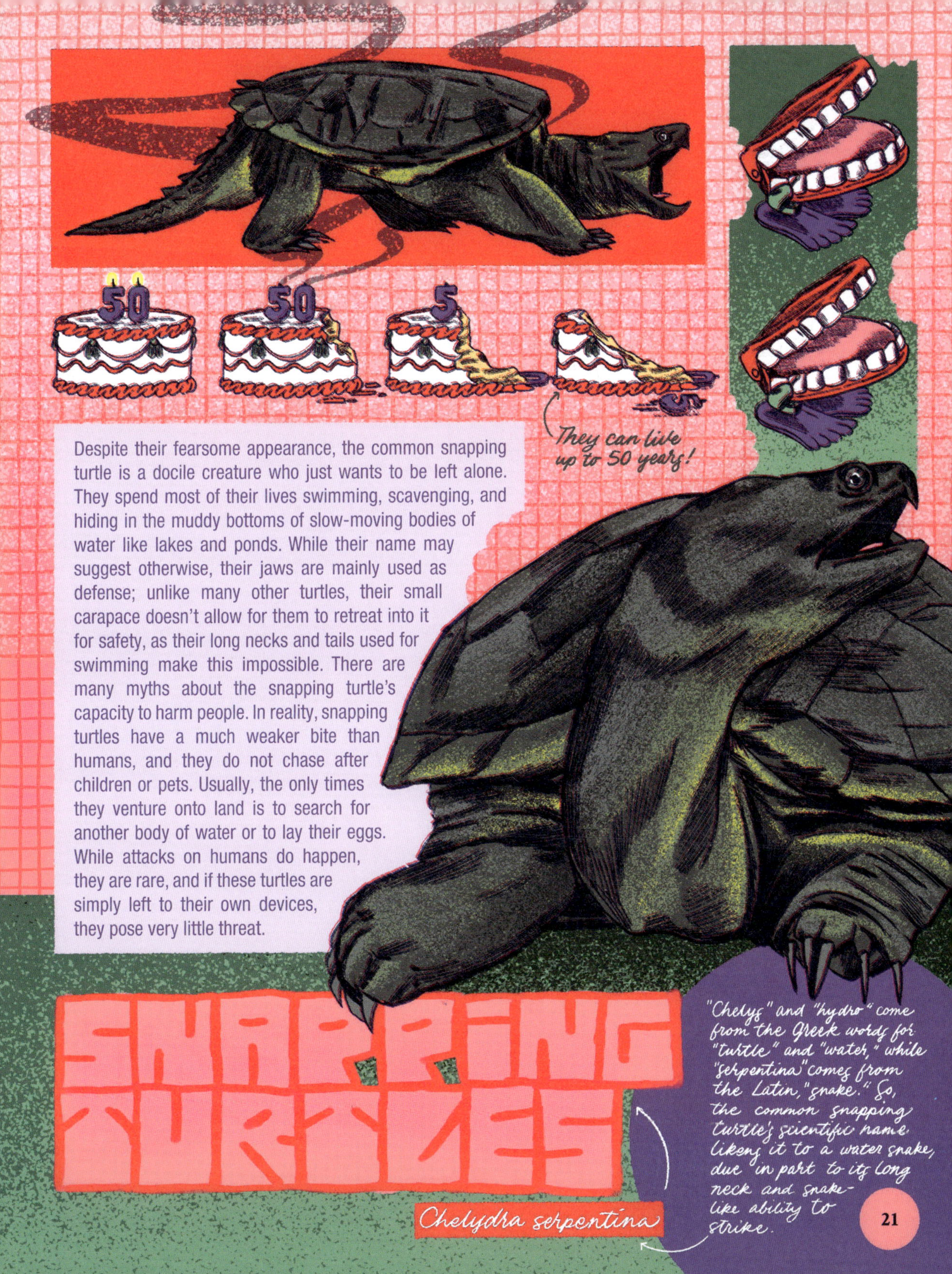

Despite their fearsome appearance, the common snapping turtle is a docile creature who just wants to be left alone. They spend most of their lives swimming, scavenging, and hiding in the muddy bottoms of slow-moving bodies of water like lakes and ponds. While their name may suggest otherwise, their jaws are mainly used as defense; unlike many other turtles, their small carapace doesn't allow for them to retreat into it for safety, as their long necks and tails used for swimming make this impossible. There are many myths about the snapping turtle's capacity to harm people. In reality, snapping turtles have a much weaker bite than humans, and they do not chase after children or pets. Usually, the only times they venture onto land is to search for another body of water or to lay their eggs. While attacks on humans do happen, they are rare, and if these turtles are simply left to their own devices, they pose very little threat.

SNAPPING TURTLES

Chelydra serpentina

"Chelys" and "hydro" come from the Greek words for "turtle" and "water," while "serpentina" comes from the Latin, "snake." So, the common snapping turtle's scientific name likens it to a water snake, due in part to its long neck and snake-like ability to strike.

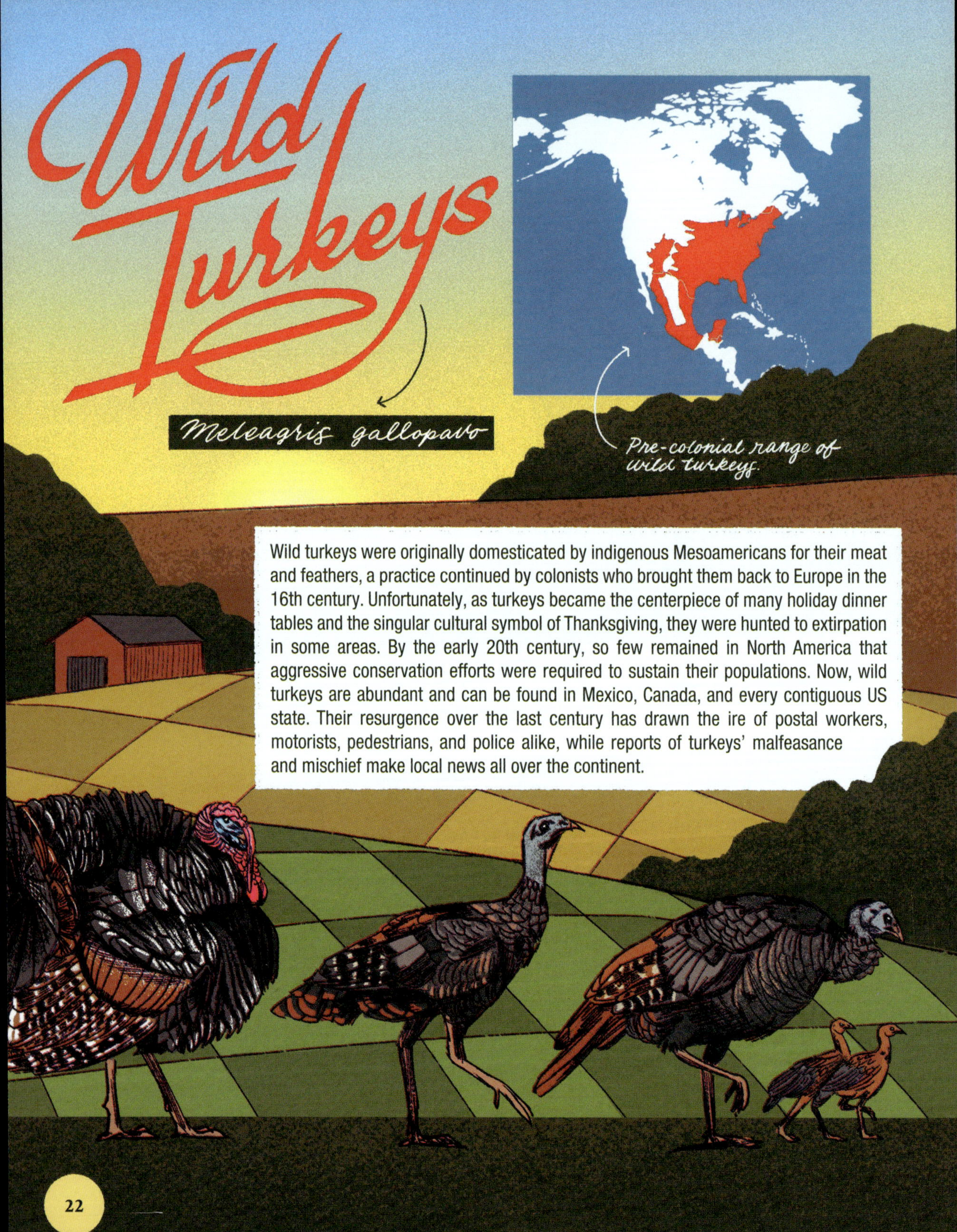

Wild turkeys were originally domesticated by indigenous Mesoamericans for their meat and feathers, a practice continued by colonists who brought them back to Europe in the 16th century. Unfortunately, as turkeys became the centerpiece of many holiday dinner tables and the singular cultural symbol of Thanksgiving, they were hunted to extirpation in some areas. By the early 20th century, so few remained in North America that aggressive conservation efforts were required to sustain their populations. Now, wild turkeys are abundant and can be found in Mexico, Canada, and every contiguous US state. Their resurgence over the last century has drawn the ire of postal workers, motorists, pedestrians, and police alike, while reports of turkeys' malfeasance and mischief make local news all over the continent.

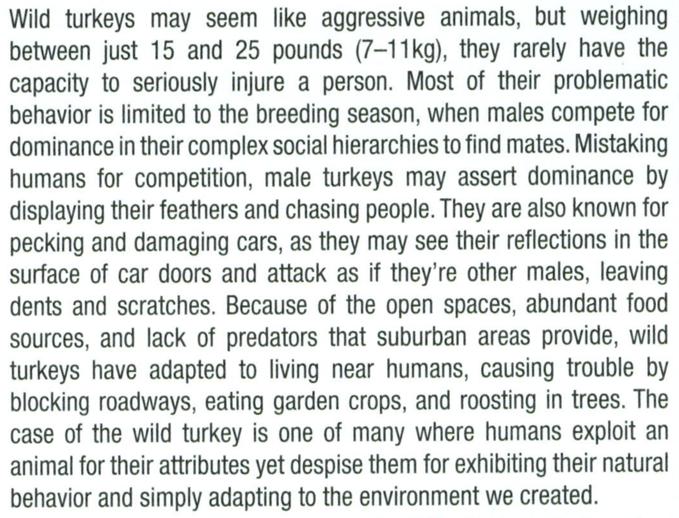

Wild turkeys may seem like aggressive animals, but weighing between just 15 and 25 pounds (7–11kg), they rarely have the capacity to seriously injure a person. Most of their problematic behavior is limited to the breeding season, when males compete for dominance in their complex social hierarchies to find mates. Mistaking humans for competition, male turkeys may assert dominance by displaying their feathers and chasing people. They are also known for pecking and damaging cars, as they may see their reflections in the surface of car doors and attack as if they're other males, leaving dents and scratches. Because of the open spaces, abundant food sources, and lack of predators that suburban areas provide, wild turkeys have adapted to living near humans, causing trouble by blocking roadways, eating garden crops, and roosting in trees. The case of the wild turkey is one of many where humans exploit an animal for their attributes yet despise them for exhibiting their natural behavior and simply adapting to the environment we created.

Turkeys have historically been revered by Indigenous peoples throughout North America. There is archaeological evidence of turkeys receiving ceremonial burials in present-day Colorado over a thousand years ago, with no indication they had been eaten. Indigenous peoples also made blankets adorned with turkey feathers.

Ben Franklin was fond of turkeys, but he never advocated for them to be the national symbol of the United States, despite widespread belief.

Turkeys' snoods grow longer as they age.

Garter Snakes

Thamnophis sirtalis

The common garter snake (named after men's sock garters, which typically shared the animal's three bright stripes) is one of the most common and abundant snakes in North America. These versatile reptiles adapted well to living around humans, especially in suburban settings in the Northeast, where there are plenty of backyard gardens. While snakes are feared and hated by many people across the globe, this small and harmless species is often persecuted and mislabeled as a pest or danger. Nonetheless dubbed the gardener's best friend, the garter snake doesn't bite unless threatened or handled, and their venom is nontoxic to people who don't have a specific allergy to it. They are shy, mostly solitary animals who provide great benefits to gardeners looking to grow a variety of plants. Their diet includes slugs, sow bugs, squash bugs, cucumber beetles, invasive Japanese beetle larvae, meadow voles, and other animals likely to chew through a gardener's favorite plants.

Garter snakes are harmless helpers playing an important role in the ecosystem and food chain. Frustrated gardeners often use pesticides to protect their plants, and inadvertently poison these innocuous and beneficial animals. Unfortunately, the use of these harmful chemicals has significantly reduced the population of this otherwise successful and resilient species. Because the common garter snake is a low-level predator, other predators who eat garter snakes (including foxes, hawks, raccoons, bullfrogs, and great blue herons) may also become poisoned from having eaten the offending garter snake. In turn, when we think we're simply protecting our tomato plants from thieving freeloaders, we may unknowingly be killing more undeserving animals than we might think. Welcoming garter snakes into our gardens not only helps our plants thrive, but it also helps backyard ecosystems remain in harmony.

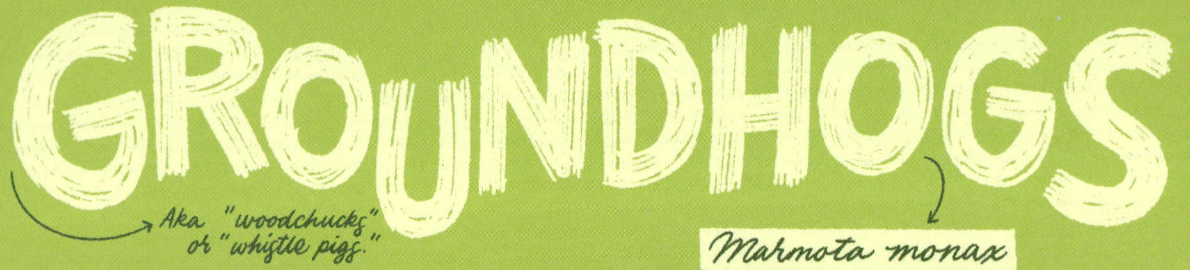

GROUNDHOGS

Aka "woodchucks" or "whistle pigs."

Marmota monax

Groundhogs are mythologized as mammalian meteorologists and garden destroyers, but the truth about them is much more complicated. The folklore surrounding Groundhog Day is thought to date back to pagan Europe, and eventually Germanic celebrations foretelling the beginning of spring, where it was believed that the badger could predict the start of the season. Centuries later in Pennsylvania, the European badger was replaced by the native groundhog, and a kitschier, more secular version of the holiday was born. While groundhogs can't predict the weather the way Punxsutawney Phil is folklorized to, they have proven to be bellwethers for a changing climate. Scientists studying groundhogs cite their shortening winter hibernation periods as a stark warning of a warming planet, which is bad news for groundhogs and humans alike.

They eat dandelions!

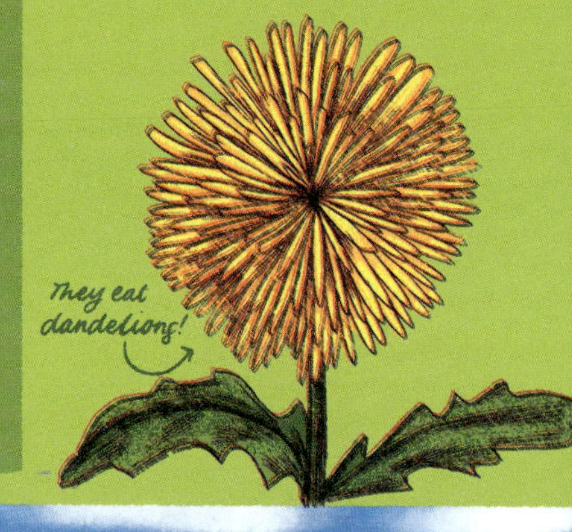

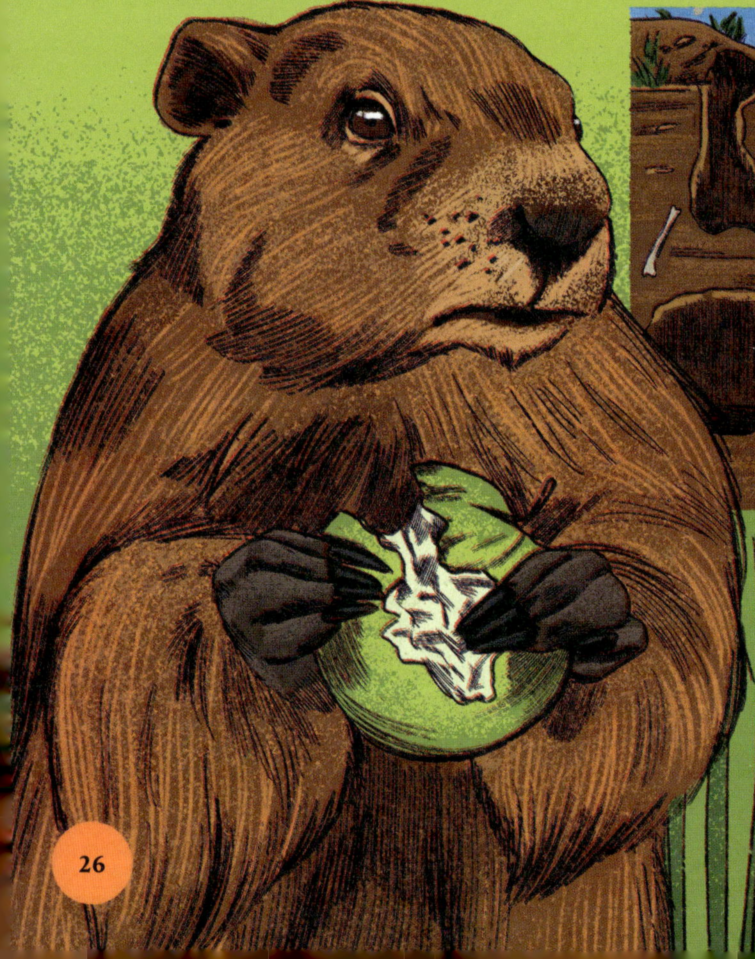

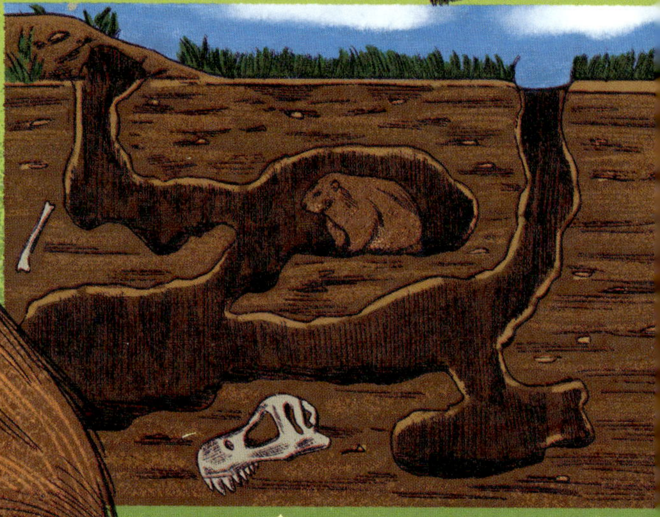
Groundhog burrows are complex structures that have multiple entrances and dedicated "rooms" for sleeping, nursing, and waste.

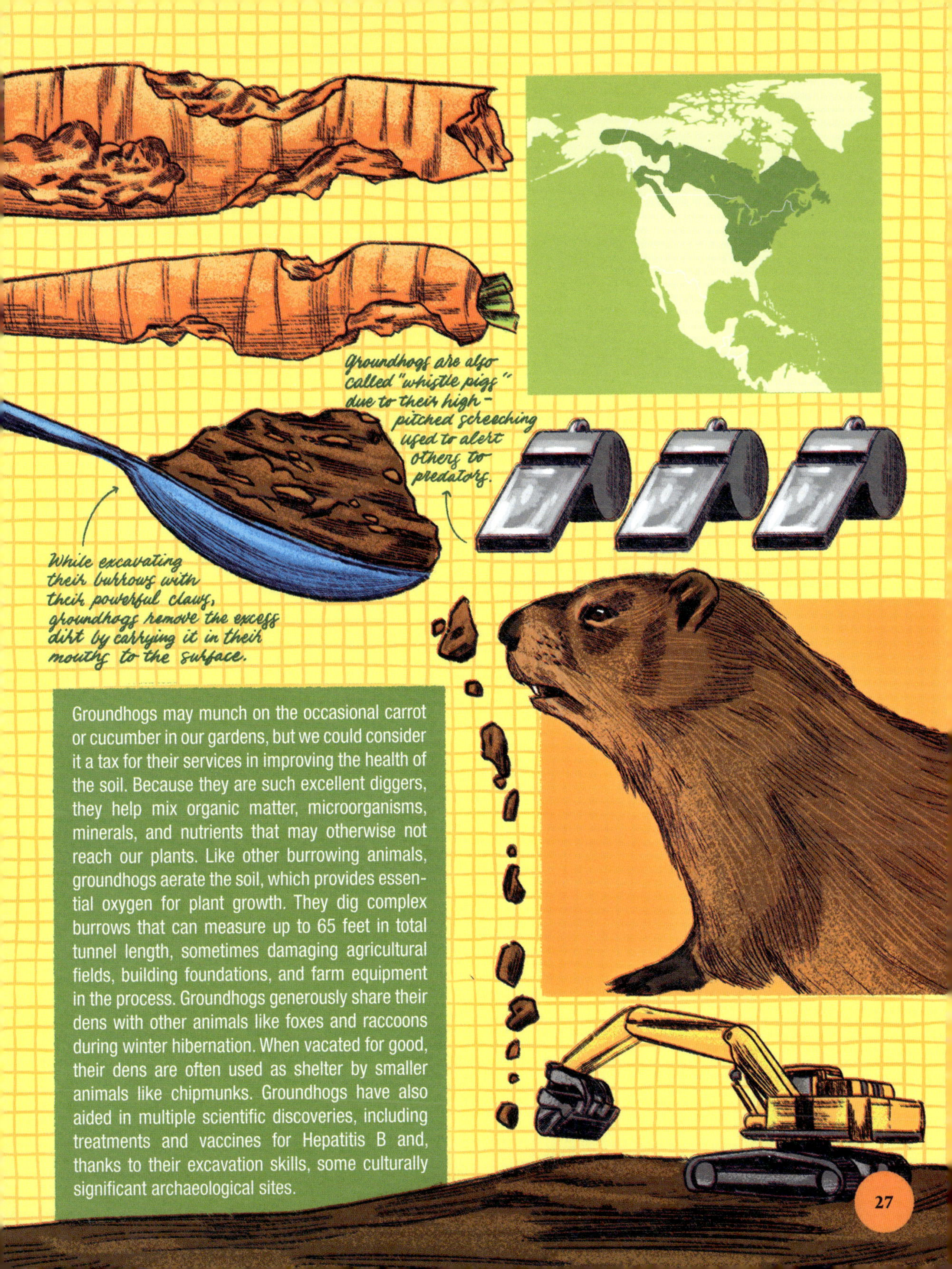

Groundhogs may munch on the occasional carrot or cucumber in our gardens, but we could consider it a tax for their services in improving the health of the soil. Because they are such excellent diggers, they help mix organic matter, microorganisms, minerals, and nutrients that may otherwise not reach our plants. Like other burrowing animals, groundhogs aerate the soil, which provides essential oxygen for plant growth. They dig complex burrows that can measure up to 65 feet in total tunnel length, sometimes damaging agricultural fields, building foundations, and farm equipment in the process. Groundhogs generously share their dens with other animals like foxes and raccoons during winter hibernation. When vacated for good, their dens are often used as shelter by smaller animals like chipmunks. Groundhogs have also aided in multiple scientific discoveries, including treatments and vaccines for Hepatitis B and, thanks to their excavation skills, some culturally significant archaeological sites.

From the
Deep South
SOUT

EAST
to the Florida Peninsula

Alligators

Alligators are among the most formidable predators in the world. These ancient reptiles are native to the coastal southeastern United States and have remained relatively unchanged for eight million years. In Florida, the alligator population stands at 1.3 million individuals: that's roughly one alligator for every 16 people living in the state. After being hunted to near extinction in the early 1900s, officials successfully implemented conservation programs, significantly boosting the population of this iconic living fossil. Of course, the sight of an alligator might strike fear in even the most avid animal lover, but the odds of being seriously injured by one (about one in three million) are less than those of being struck by lightning. In Florida, there has been an average of only eight attacks each year, likely the result of "nuisance alligators" who have lost their natural fear of humans due to being deliberately fed by them. Feeding alligators is a misdemeanor in Florida and Texas for a reason.

What defines "nuisance alligators" is relatively vague, however. In Florida, they must be at least four feet in length and "pose a threat to people, pets, or property," while in Texas, an alligator who kills livestock or is otherwise a "threat to human health or safety" makes the grade. States even offer hotlines for residents to report alligators. In Florida, the majority of these calls result in permits being issued to kill them. Sadly, many such complaints refer to alligators who are simply existing near people as a consequence of habitat loss and human development. As a result, nearly 200,000 alligators have been killed by permitted trappers in Florida since the 1990s, many of whom were sold to meat processors. Despite the danger alligators can pose to humans, their right to exist in their natural habitat remains. Alligators are valuable predators who are critical to these fragile ecosystems; they even help control the populations of invasive pythons in the Florida Everglades, a persistent problem created by the human introduction of a lethal, non-native species. When appreciated from afar, these animals' true nature shines. They are powerful, intelligent, and curious creatures who deserve to be left in peace.

Peacocks

Pavo cristatus

Blue peacocks are native to India, but have been the object of international trade for millennia. Their populations in North America are comprised of escaped feral individuals (and their descendants) who were purchased as pets or for ornamental purposes, often by hotels, resorts, and golf courses. Humans love their iridescent feathers, of course, but peacocks are also known for ripping roof shingles off buildings, shattering windows, damaging cars, and decapitating flowers. Their loud vocalizations that occur day and night are the subject of noise complaints by residents. Like wild turkeys, most of peacocks' destructive behavior is limited to mating season. People either love them or hate them; some enjoy them for their aesthetic qualities, while others shoot, poison, and intentionally run them over for one offense or another. Experts say that peacocks are unlikely to threaten the ecosystems where they've been introduced, so we'd do well to overlook their trespasses, appreciate their exotic charm, and let them be. After all, if they're somewhere they shouldn't be, it's because of us.

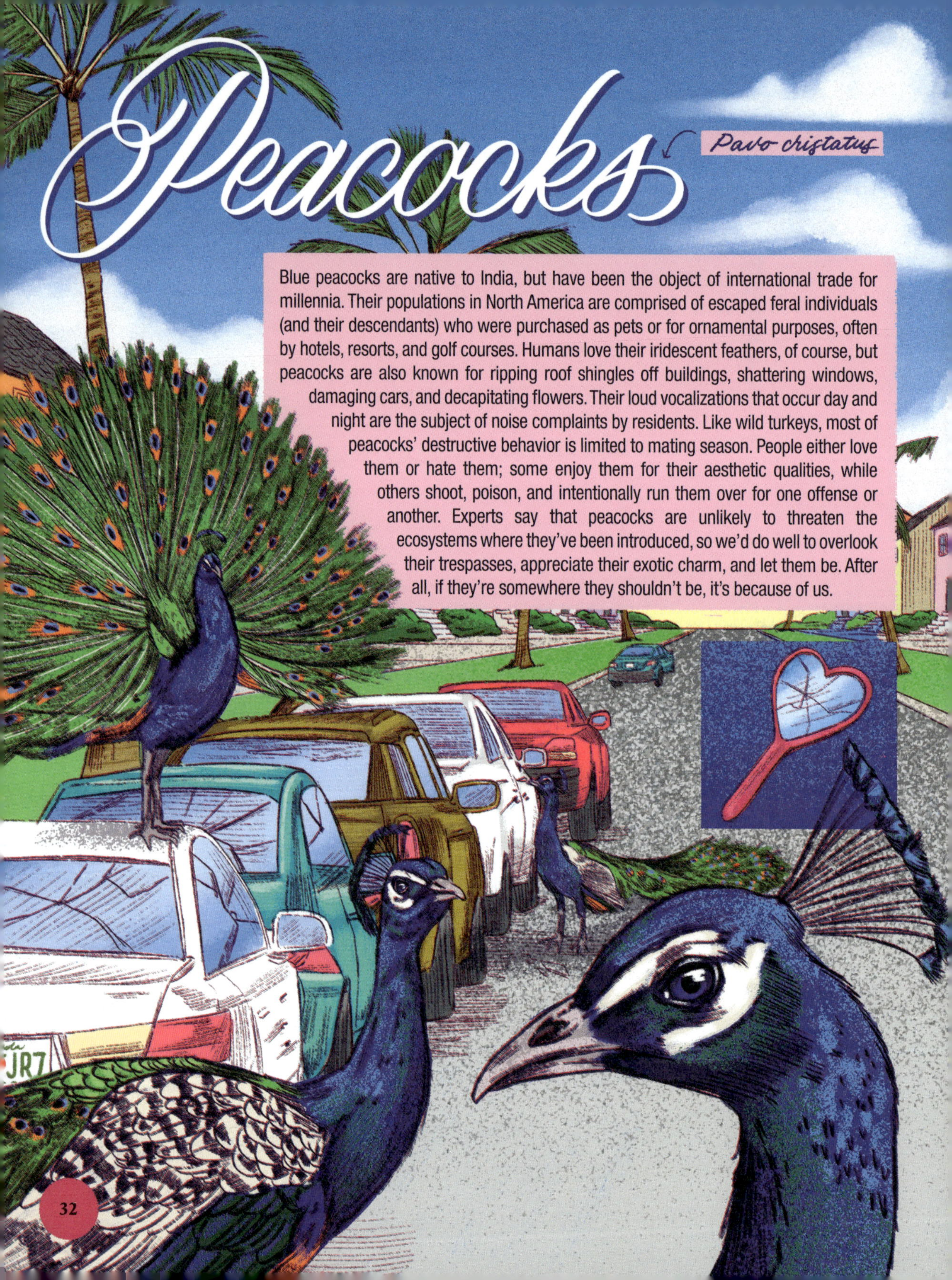

MUSCOVY DUCKS

Cairina moschata

Muscovy ducks are one of only two native North American birds that have been domesticated (the other being the wild turkey). While their range includes Central and South America, as well as parts of coastal Texas, domesticated Muscovy ducks were introduced to Florida in the 1960s. Many escaped captivity, and feral populations boomed. Like peacocks, their presence is divisive. Because Muscovies are prolific, year-round breeders who tend to favor suburban environments, they are considered a nuisance by many, primarily for soiling driveways, yards, and cars with their waste. Sadly, they're also maligned simply for their unusually warty appearance. While considered invasive, these otherwise sociable, docile birds don't compete with native species and pose no threat to humans. Even so, Muscovy ducks are frequently the victims of heinous abuse and intentional killing that has even resulted in criminal charges.

Imported Exotic Animals

Apart from sparking concerns around animal welfare and conservation, the multi-billion-dollar global pet trade industry (legal and illegal) has introduced countless invasive species worldwide, including the Burmese python, now one of the largest ecological threats to the Florida Everglades. Originally released by or escaped from pet owners, Burmese pythons adapt well to Florida's subtropical climate and have no natural predators, so they have bred prolifically in the wild since the 1970s. Taking a wrecking ball to the food chain, they have decimated both prey and predator populations alike, as they can easily overcome deer and are known to eat young alligators, too. Florida has implemented a number of programs to combat Burmese pythons. The Exotic Pet Amnesty Program allows residents to surrender illegal exotic pets free of penalty. The Python Elimination Program and the annual Python Challenge incentivize residents to kill them by offering payment and prizes in exchange for python carcasses.

Experts warn that the next invasive threat could be the tegu lizard, another victim of the pet trade. These hardy reptiles are known to eat the eggs of alligators and ecologically threatened gopher tortoises; their current population in Florida is unknown, but it is on ecologists' radar. Without increased regulation of the pet industry, the stories of these species are doomed to be repeated in a cascade of ecological crises, which are only exacerbated by climate change. An astonishing 50 percent of all pets in the U.S. are considered exotic, and the demand for these animals has only increased. It is easy to cast blame on these so-called invaders, but like the ecosystems they harm, they are victims of our culture's materialism.

Cane Toads

Rhinella marina

Cane toads were deliberately introduced in Florida in the 1930s to combat sugar cane crop pests. Today, these humongous toads overrun gardens and poison predators and pets alike with their toxic skin secretions.

Red-Eared Sliders

Trachemys scripta elegans

Red-eared sliders have established invasive populations in every U.S. state except Alaska due to the pet trade. They routinely outcompete native aquatic turtles for prey and habitat. Like the Burmese python and others, they can be rehomed with Florida's Exotic Pet Amnesty Program.

Rhesus Macaques

Macaca mulatta

Rhesus macaques were introduced to Florida in the 1930s by Colonel S. Tooey, the owner of Silver Springs Nature Theme Park, famous for its glass-bottom boat tours along the Silver River. Mistakenly thinking they couldn't swim, Tooey released six macaques onto an island in the river to help attract tourists. Since then, the monkeys have established a sizable population of around 600 individuals that extends far beyond the original boundaries of the attraction, now a state park. Various attempts to humanely manage the population through sterilization had little effect. The macaques have since become habituated to humans due to illegal feeding and still draw tourists to the park despite their habit of stealing food and jumping onto pontoon tour boats. Unfortunately, a large portion of the monkeys are thought to carry the herpes B virus, which, while unlikely, can spread to humans, but only through bites and scratches.

Capybaras

Hydrochoerus hydrochaeris

Having escaped a research lab in Northern Florida in the 1990s, capybaras have established a small population of approximately 50 individuals in the area, sparking concern among ecologists.

AMERICAN GREEN Tree Frogs

Hyla cinerea

Abundant in urban and suburban environments, the American green tree frog is often found on sliding glass doors, windows, and siding. They have specialized toes for gripping, and their skin secretes a sticky mucus that allows them to climb virtually any surface, which is why they show up in places some would rather they didn't. At night, they congregate near porch lights, which attract a smorgasbord of insects (including pesky mosquitoes), in search of their next meal. To the chagrin of light sleepers, they emit loud vocalizations, especially at night, in search of mates. These small but mighty frogs may be an unwelcome presence to some, but they are insatiable insect eaters that play a role in the health of ecosystems and our gardens.

GREEN IGUANAS

Iguana iguana

Native to Central and South America and parts of the Caribbean, green iguanas are considered invasive in Florida. Their populations have become so abundant that they threaten native species like the endangered Miami blue butterfly. As is the case with most non-native reptiles in the state, experts believe their persistent growth is a direct result of the pet trade—iguanas made up nearly half of all reptiles bought and sold in the U.S. between 1996 and 2012. Ecological concern is often overshadowed, though, given the iguana's propensity to eat ornamental plants and flowers, spark power outages (28 in 2020 alone) when climbing on transformers, and swim in residential pools. Moreover, with extreme weather on the rise due to climate change, sudden and unusual cold temperatures cause iguanas to enter a temporary state of torpor, which can cause them to fall from trees, sometimes injuring people and damaging cars. It is legal to kill iguanas without a permit on private property and some public lands in Florida. Ecologists and animal rights activists warn that without a significant crackdown on the pet industry, the indiscriminate and unregulated killing of these animals results in cruelty and fails to address the root cause. Thankfully, the state passed a law in 2021 banning the sale and possession of live iguanas, a step in the right, humane direction.

Herons + Egrets

Great blue herons and great egrets are large, mostly piscivorous birds known for their elegant features. Both are notorious in the commercial fishing industry for hunting prey at aquaculture facilities such as bait fish farms and sport fisheries. They tend to frequent these sites as fish are artificially made abundant there, providing them with easy prey. Studies show that despite these habits, the net yield of these enterprises remains largely unaffected because wading birds tend to prey on sick fish who linger at the water's surface. Deriding these animals for seeking out an easy meal while we simultaneously degrade their habitat due to climate change and development is illogical and irresponsible, but all too typical.

In addition to being perceived as freeloaders, herons and egrets are the subject of many civilian complaints. They breed in large groups, which can be noisy, disrupt commercial flight patterns, and generate large amounts of droppings, sparking what experts call overblown fears of disease transmission. Great blue herons are also known to dine on unsuspecting koi in ornamental ponds. Despite all of this, we can thank these birds for playing a critical role in the early stages of the conservation movement in the United States. In the 19th century, when feathered hats were all the rage, plume hunting was extremely profitable and responsible for millions of bird deaths, including great blue herons and great egrets. At the time, egret feathers were worth $32 per ounce (around $1,200 today), which was double the price of gold at the time. In 1910, the first Audubon Society chapter helped pass laws restricting the practice. As the movement gained momentum, the great egret became the symbol of the newly formed National Audubon Society, whose efforts ultimately contributed to the passage of the Migratory Bird Treaty Act of 1918. Buttressed by international treaties with Canada, this law continues to protect all native birds from a variety of human threats.

Armadillos

Dasypus novemcinctus

Armadillos' preferred meal is insects—they love to dig up ants, termites, and grubs using their sharp claws, spotting where they could be with their keen sense of smell.

The nine-banded armadillo is one of over 20 species of armadillos on Earth, but the only one native to North America. These armored, cat-sized mammals have expanded their range north and east of their original territory of Central and South America over the last few centuries. Because of climate change and human development driving out most of their predators, armadillo populations have flourished. They've been branded as nuisances thanks to their propensity to dig small, narrow burrows in places that farmers and suburbanites alike would prefer they avoid entirely. Along with their scaly appearance, the armadillo has poor eyesight, tending to bump into things (and people) as its nose remains fixed to the ground for foraging. As with the box turtle, some even refer to them as "speed bumps," since their poor eyesight lands them in the middle of roads where they are frequently targeted. Aside from humans, armadillos are the only known species that are able to contract leprosy, which further contributes to their bad reputation. However, the risk of a leprosy infection from human-armadillo contact remains extremely low.

Armadillos are harmless to humans and beneficial to other animals; they help support the survival of over 60 other species in their range, such as burrowing owls and bobcats. Like the groundhog, armadillo burrows are reused by many animals to store food, give birth, and provide shelter from weather and predators. Because of human development and the subsequent habitat loss of countless species, the armadillo's contributions are particularly valuable in sustaining biodiversity and ecological equilibrium. As primarily insectivorous mammals, they consume many dangerous or otherwise unwanted animals like scorpions, fire ants, yellowjackets, cockroaches, and grubs. In addition to being helpful, armadillos are fascinating in their own right. The Aztec word for armadillo translates roughly to "turtle rabbit," which is quite apt given that they are the only mammal that has a carapace. Confounding evolutionary biologists, armadillos always give birth to identical quadruplets—the only known vertebrate to do so. Despite the minor inconveniences armadillos may cause, these unique animals are essential and must be preserved.

From the Four

THI
ST
ners to Mexico

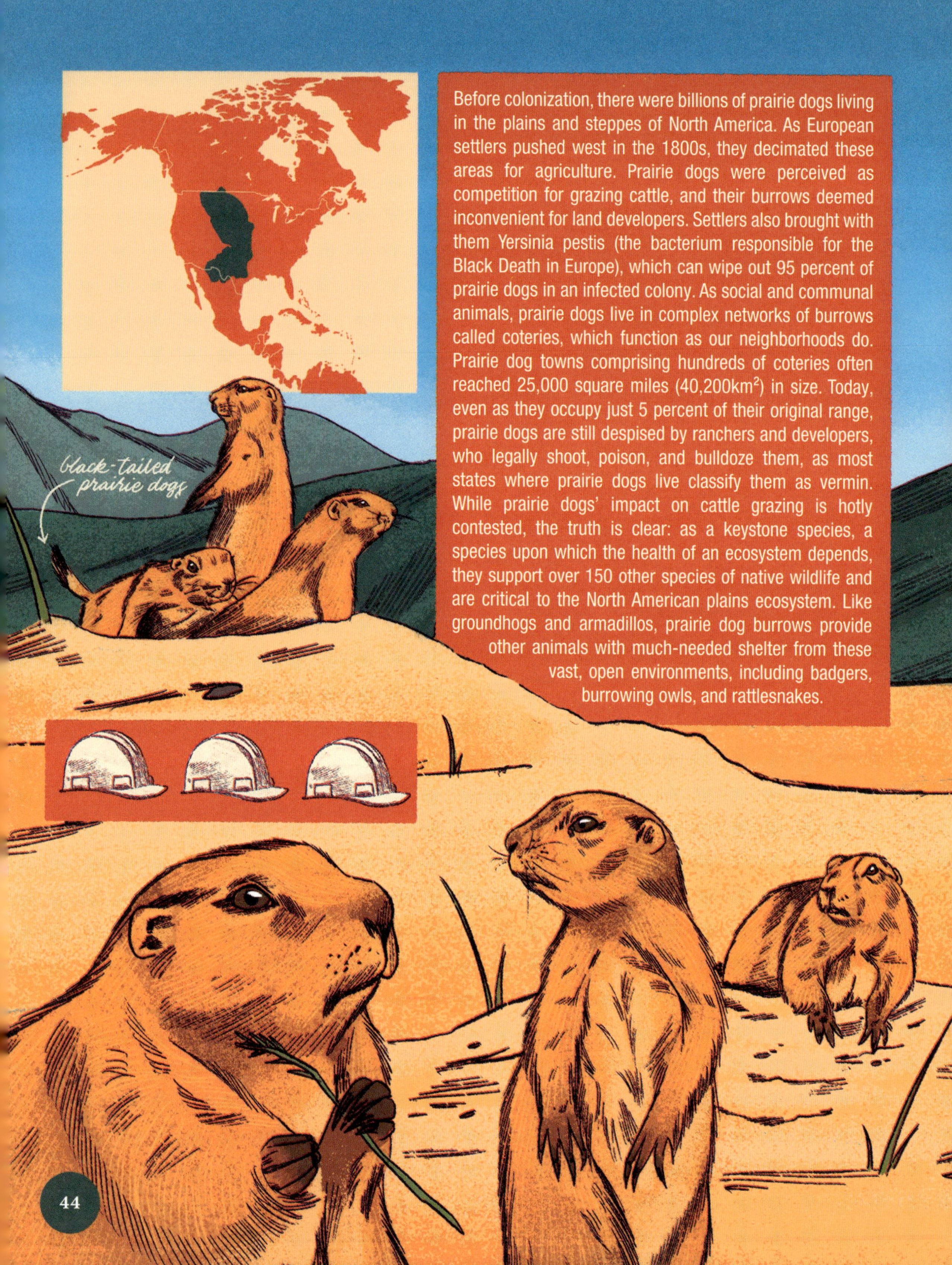

Before colonization, there were billions of prairie dogs living in the plains and steppes of North America. As European settlers pushed west in the 1800s, they decimated these areas for agriculture. Prairie dogs were perceived as competition for grazing cattle, and their burrows deemed inconvenient for land developers. Settlers also brought with them Yersinia pestis (the bacterium responsible for the Black Death in Europe), which can wipe out 95 percent of prairie dogs in an infected colony. As social and communal animals, prairie dogs live in complex networks of burrows called coteries, which function as our neighborhoods do. Prairie dog towns comprising hundreds of coteries often reached 25,000 square miles (40,200km^2) in size. Today, even as they occupy just 5 percent of their original range, prairie dogs are still despised by ranchers and developers, who legally shoot, poison, and bulldoze them, as most states where prairie dogs live classify them as vermin. While prairie dogs' impact on cattle grazing is hotly contested, the truth is clear: as a keystone species, a species upon which the health of an ecosystem depends, they support over 150 other species of native wildlife and are critical to the North American plains ecosystem. Like groundhogs and armadillos, prairie dog burrows provide other animals with much-needed shelter from these vast, open environments, including badgers, burrowing owls, and rattlesnakes.

Prairie dogs are prey for many other species, too, both by land and airborne. They maintain the grasses surrounding their burrows at a height of six inches (15cm) or less, strategic eating that allows them to see predators more easily. Moreover, prairie dogs' fastidious landscaping supports declining grassland birds like the near-threatened mountain plovers, who prefer short grasses; their decline is a direct result of the loss of prairie dog colonies. Peeking out of their burrows on their hind legs, prairie dogs emit distinct vocalizations to warn of various predators. The long-billed curlew, a ground-nesting prairie bird, is known to eavesdrop on these warnings, saving them from certain death. The survival of the endangered black-footed ferret hinges entirely on that of prairie dogs, which make up 90 percent of their diet. While we may find these small, burrowing rodents at times inconvenient, prairie dogs are sophisticated, social animals who are critical to the stability of the environment. It's clear that when prairie dogs are doing well, so is everyone else. In protecting them, we protect our future, too.

JAVELINAS

Aka "skunk pigs" or "peccaries."

Pecari tajacu

Despite their appearance, javelinas are not closely related to pigs; rather, they belong to a family called peccaries. As a result of colonization's effect on native grasses, these short, near-sighted animals have expanded their range north from Central America over the last 250 years. Considered a nuisance and often mistaken for feral pigs or wild boars, javelina populations have declined due to recreational hunting and removal by killing and relocation. They're herd animals that travel in groups of around ten and are often seen digging up flower beds or eating ornamental cacti in yards and gardens. Usually, they approach man-made structures in search of food, shade, or warmth, and will move on quickly. The colloquial name for the collared peccary, "javelina," comes from the Spanish jabalina, or javelin, alluding to their razor-sharp teeth. They are harmless if unprovoked but may accidentally bite when being fed by well-meaning but misguided humans.

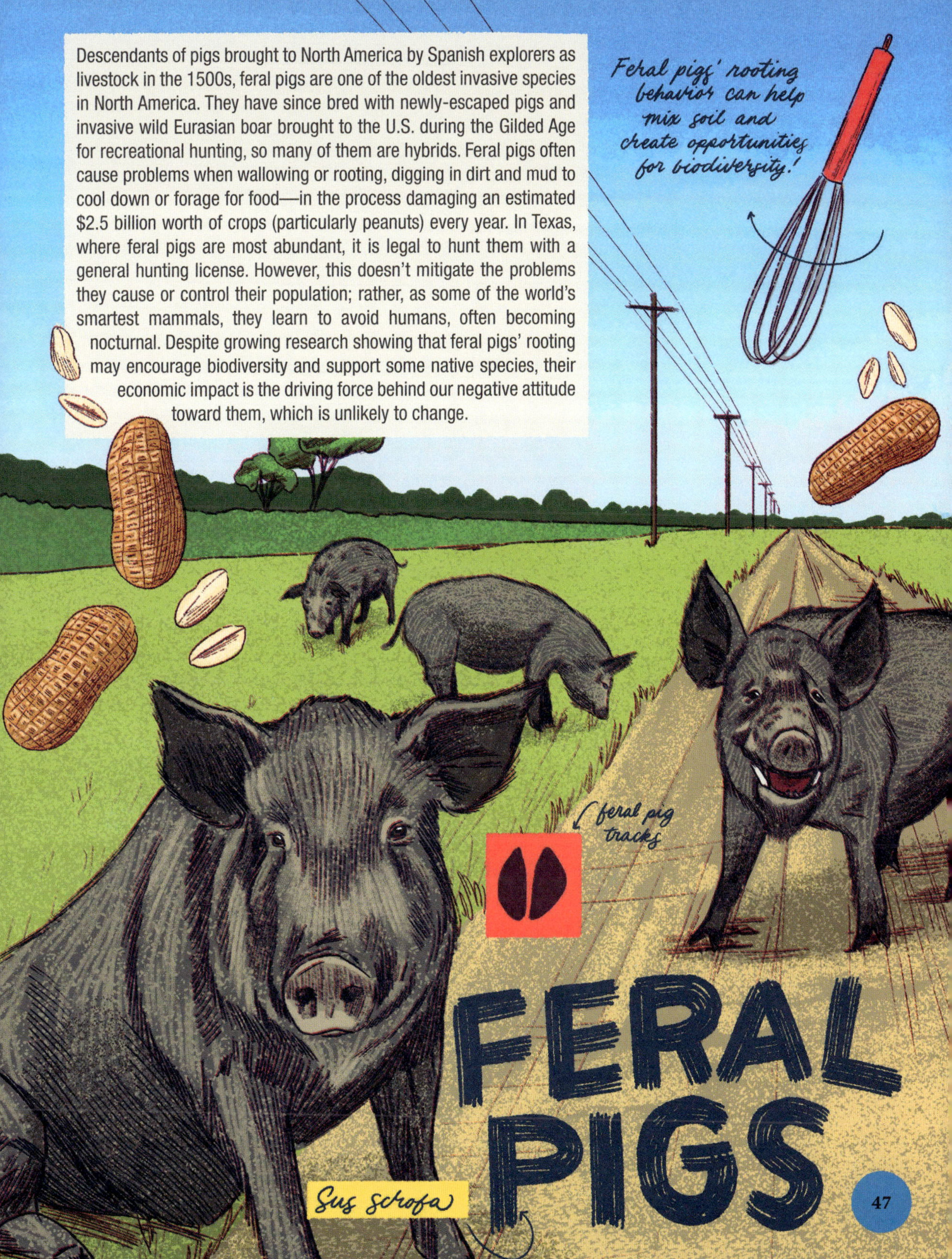

Descendants of pigs brought to North America by Spanish explorers as livestock in the 1500s, feral pigs are one of the oldest invasive species in North America. They have since bred with newly-escaped pigs and invasive wild Eurasian boar brought to the U.S. during the Gilded Age for recreational hunting, so many of them are hybrids. Feral pigs often cause problems when wallowing or rooting, digging in dirt and mud to cool down or forage for food—in the process damaging an estimated $2.5 billion worth of crops (particularly peanuts) every year. In Texas, where feral pigs are most abundant, it is legal to hunt them with a general hunting license. However, this doesn't mitigate the problems they cause or control their population; rather, as some of the world's smartest mammals, they learn to avoid humans, often becoming nocturnal. Despite growing research showing that feral pigs' rooting may encourage biodiversity and support some native species, their economic impact is the driving force behind our negative attitude toward them, which is unlikely to change.

Bats

Despite being helpful to humanity and the ecosystem, bats are haunted by ghoulish cultural signifiers and outright myths that make us fear and hate them. Roosting in buildings during warmer months, they draw the ire of homeowners, as most bats can squeeze into holes less than an inch (2.5cm) wide. This becomes a problem when they make noise or leave droppings that accumulate in attics, garages, and crawlspaces. Many bats are migratory, so our attics might just be a pit stop on their long journeys from which they'll likely move on quickly. To make matters worse for bats, it is a widespread misconception that they routinely spread rabies. Notwithstanding, less than 0.5 percent of bats even carry the disease, and the average person's risk of contracting rabies from a bat is extremely low. Interestingly enough, rabies was first introduced to North America by domestic dogs.

Mexican free-tailed bat (Tadarida brasiliensis)

It wasn't until after the European colonization of the Americas that bats became culturally synonymous with vampires. That's because the only sanguivorous, or blood-drinking, bats in the world live in the Western Hemisphere.

Congress Avenue Bridge, located in Austin, Texas, is home to 1.5 million Mexican free-tailed bats, making it the site of the largest urban bat colony on the planet. The bridge draws over a hundred thousand tourists each year.

People accuse bats of divebombing them, but they're usually just going after the insects that people attract. Most bats are insatiable insectivores; they can consume more than half their body weight in insects each night. Some use echolocation to identify their prey, catching insects in their mouths mid-air. Consequently, they are frequent predators of crop pests. Mexican free-tailed bats fly at speeds up to 99.4 miles per hour (160kph), making them the fastest mammal on Earth. During these speedy flights, they prey on the corn earworm moth and tobacco budworm moth. Additionally, the big brown bat is a predator of the corn rootworm, one of the most destructive crop pests on the continent. Some bats are even fruit pollinators, responsible for pollinating over 300 different fruits!

BLACK-TAILED JACKRABBITS

Lepus californicus

Black-tailed jackrabbits are known throughout the American Southwest and Mexico as notorious crop thieves because they damage trees, orchards, and other agricultural assets as they forage for food. Over the last few centuries, European settlers hunted and trapped a huge number of their natural predators, resulting in a population boom of jackrabbits. At the same time, their habitats have been reduced by human development and agricultural land use. Jackrabbits get most of the water they need from the shrubs they eat, so they can thrive in harsh, arid environments. They rest in small depressions in the soil rather than dens, which provides visibility across the vast plains they live in, essential to spot predators. Their acute eyesight and hearing serve as the first line of defense in these open environments, augmented by their incredible speed and agility. As with so many animals we consider nuisances, it's essential to understand that by retooling the environment for our needs, we've created an inherent conflict between our convenience and their survival.

RATTLESNAKES

North America is home to over 30 species of rattlesnakes, and they are feared for their potentially fatal, venomous bites. As reclusive animals, rattlesnake bites occur usually on human hands, feet, and ankles when people accidentally step on or near the snakes. While they warn of a potential attack with their specialized tail for which they're named, rattlesnakes can be hard for cyclists and hikers to spot due to their camouflaged skin. If given a wide berth, rattlesnakes will usually retreat rather than attack. While rattlesnakes present valid safety concerns for humans, the fear surrounding them is often overblown. Of the approximately 8,000 rattlesnake bites that occur in the U.S. each year, only five are fatal, usually due to a lack of proper treatment. Rattlesnakes also occupy an important ecological niche. They excel at controlling rodent populations, which are often overly abundant near human population centers. Each rattlesnake consumes over 20 rodents per year. Additionally, researchers have discovered that the toxin in rattlesnake venom (crotoxin) could be used to treat chronic pain and play a significant role in cancer treatment.

WHITE-NOSED Coatis

Nasua narica

Coatis are small mammals related to raccoons and have garnered a similar reputation. They are known to predate on chickens, break into garbage cans (and houses), and even damage fruit crops in search of food. Unlike raccoons, however, coatis are diurnal, meaning they are active during the day. They live in many areas frequented by tourists who, thinking they're cute critters, often feed them. As is the case with most wildlife, however, when humans feed coatis, they lose their fear of us and can become aggressive. Coatis have an excellent memory and sense of smell, so once they're habituated to being fed, it can be difficult to prevent them from returning. They tend to travel in large groups, so they can easily overwhelm resorts and towns where they settle.

Coatis are legally hunted in nearly every jurisdiction in which they live. Often accompanied by dogs, hunters deride coatis as aggressive because they are known to injure the dogs when cornered. Regardless of what people think of coatis, their "undesirable" behavior is once again a result of human activity. Whether it's human development encroaching on their habitats, expansion of their range north due to climate change, or breaking into improperly secured garbage, coatis are simply adapting to an environment dominated by humans. We might instead look to what they do for the planet in spite of us: namely, as omnivores who prefer fruit, they function as seed dispersers as well as pest control, using their powerful claws and flexible noses to root out insects.

WE

From the Great Plains
to the Pacific

Sandhill cranes are large migratory birds that are the enemies of farmers across the Midwest and Great Plains. Flocking in groups as large as 100 birds, they frequently dine on corn seeds in spring, a single crane eating up to 800 corn kernels per day. They're also known for damaging crops of potatoes and grains. Despite experiencing a significant dip in the early 20th century, sandhill crane populations have boomed since the 1980s. The degradation of wetlands and increase of agricultural development has forced them to adapt to foraging in fields, which they recall and revisit yearly during migration, increasing farmers' disdain for them.

While farmers may find them gluttonous nuisances, sandhill cranes compensate for at least some of what they take by eating waste grain and crop pests like beetles, larvae, and the occasional rodent. Unfortunately, despite being protected by the Migratory Bird Treaty Act, regulated hunting of sandhill cranes is legal in 15 states in the U.S. They are also occasional victims of aircraft collision, as are too many migratory birds. However, as some of the oldest birds on the planet, (2.5 million years by some estimates) sandhill cranes are resilient despite the hostility, changing climate, and habitat degradation we inflict on them. The least we can do is share the spoils of our dominance.

Mountain Lions

Puma concolor

Mountain lions are condemned for killing livestock in rural areas near their natural habitats. However, farmers lose nine times more animals to disease, weather, and other factors than to all predators combined. If that's not enough to exonerate them, domestic dogs kill 35 percent more livestock than mountain lions. Perhaps more concerning is that even though mountain lions are a keystone species, they are often the target of legal trophy hunting by wealthy tourists. An estimated 500 mountain lions are killed in Colorado each year by trophy hunters, which often leaves their kittens to die of dehydration and exposure. Had it passed in the 2024 election, Colorado's ballot initiative Prop 127 would have prohibited the killing of big cats in the state. Despite how critical mountain lions are to the ecosystem, bottom lines and recreational hunting seem to prevail.

Coyotes

aka "American jackals" or "prairie wolves."

Translates to "barking dog."

Canis latrans

Coyotes are similarly accused of livestock and pet depredation, and are the target of recreational hunters, livestock owners, and USDA wildlife services. Around half a million coyotes are killed in the U.S. every year by poisoning, inhumane trapping, and shooting from helicopters. Four US states even offer bounties for coyote carcasses. While coyotes can play a role in livestock losses, killing coyotes only increases their populations. Their social structures rely on alpha pairs being the sole breeding pair of a group, and when one or both are killed, more coyotes compete for dominance, breed, separate, and pair again. Coyote populations have exploded over the last 50 years, expanding from their original range in the western half of North America as they've adapted to living around humans due to habitat loss and the availability of food. As is the story with countless nuisance animals, we demonize them for the very same behaviors we encourage through ecosystem engineering of our own.

BARRED OWLS

Strix varia

Barred owls are the latest scapegoat in the war against invasive species in the western U.S. As settlers colonized the great plains, new trees dotted grasslands, providing a road west for barred owls as habitat loss threatened their native range east of the Mississippi. By the 1970s, they arrived in the Pacific Northwest, and now compete with the threatened northern spotted owl, whose numbers were already in crisis due to logging in the region. Rather than addressing the spotted owl's habitat loss, the U.S. Fish and Wildlife Service plans to cull nearly 16,000 barred owls per year over the next three decades. So now, dual tragedies are unfolding, with humans as the sole perpetrators. Spotted owl populations continue to decline while barred owls pay the price for the logging industry's crimes against the planet. Some even refer to the barred owl as the first animal climate refugee. When humans are forced to escape more fires and floods each year, it's tough to blame animals for doing the same.

Barn Owls

Tyto furcata

While barn owls are the most widespread owls on the planet, they are declining in North America due to human activity. Between their silent flight, ghostly appearance, and screeches that sound like human screams, we have historically viewed barn owls as omens of death and persecute them as a consequence. As lethal predators with the best hearing of any known bird, barn owls are particularly adept at pest control and should be welcomed, especially by farmers, since they prefer open grassland or agricultural fields and prey on crop-eating rodents. Unfortunately, farmers use harmful chemicals instead that often poison the barn owls who eat the offending rodents. Rather than using pesticides, farmers could simply allow the barn owl to control rodent populations. One study even suggests that crop yields are markedly higher in areas where barn owl populations are allowed to flourish.

American badgers are formidable, opportunistic predators known for their prodigious digging. As mostly solitary mammals, they occupy territories up to 17 square miles (27km^2), throughout which they dig tunnels and burrows, some as deep as 9 feet (3m) and as long as 30 feet (9m). Their powerful webbed claws, muscular shoulders, and spade-shaped heads enable them to dig themselves below the surface in seconds. They've even been known to break through concrete, which makes them unpopular with humans, since they can cause structural damage to buildings, irrigation systems, and underground utility lines, to say nothing of gardens, patios, and fencing. Mostly nocturnal, American badgers don't often confront us directly, but their burrows can be a safety hazard; horses, cows, and humans have been known to sustain injuries by stepping into badger burrows. People who live in rural areas aren't fans of badgers because they occasionally take chickens and eggs from residential coops, too.

AMERICAN BADGERS

Taxidea taxus

Coyotes make great hunting partners for badgers, as coyotes are faster, but badgers can sneak and reach underground prey.

Badgers remain a protected species despite the damage they cause. Licenses and permits must be obtained to use lethal force against them, which is only fair because they make good neighbors, especially for farmers. Because they prefer open prairies, they often live near agricultural fields, where they prey on ground-dwelling rodents and insects that can damage crops. These powerful excavators also improve soil health, and frequently feed on carrion, preventing the spread of disease. Even rattlesnakes are no match for the American badger. All things considered, badgers are valuable animals worth keeping around.

PRONGHORNS

Aka "American antelopes," "prairie antelopes," "prong bucks," or "pronghorn antelopes."

Antilocapra americana

Prior to colonization, pronghorn populations exceeded 35 million. Today, there are just half a million pronghorns left in North America. Much of their habitat has been converted to agriculture, resulting in the reduction in their natural diet of shrubs and foliage. Pronghorns are loathed by ranchers because they compete with grazing livestock for food and eat stored hay and crops like alfalfa. Despite their remarkable speed, pronghorns can't jump the fences that are now ubiquitous in these areas. If able, they go around or under them and frequently get fatally caught in barbed wire. Fencing also disrupts their natural long migrations, causing unanticipated detours that can affect their access to food and breeding grounds.

Golden Eagles

Although majestic golden eagles are protected by three federal laws in the U.S., that doesn't mean they're spared from the nuisance label. In addition to being threatened by habitat loss, wind turbines, power lines, and cars, golden eagles are also frequently shot by ranchers who deem them a threat to their livestock. In fact, some research suggests the presence of golden eagles may actually help ranchers. While they are powerful birds whose killing capacity does include large animals, they prefer a diet of small rodents and mammals, many of whom are crop-eating culprits who compete with livestock for food. Eagles also often eat carcasses left behind by hunters, which prevents the spread of disease. Sadly, contamination by lead bullets in these carcasses poisons them, as does poison intended for coyotes.

GRAY WOLVES

Canis lupus

Only 1% of livestock deaths can be attributed to predators like wolves.

In pre-colonial days, the gray wolf occupied two thirds of the North American continent. As more land was allotted for animal agriculture as settlers forged west, wolves began to attack livestock, captive prey for them. Attitudes toward wolves quickly soured. Along with pronghorns and bison, settlers nearly eliminated the gray wolf altogether by the middle of the 20th century, with the last remaining population in the contiguous U.S. living in northeastern Minnesota. Today, wolves remain at the center of controversy. At the behest of the powerful livestock lobby, the U.S. Department of Agriculture has been grossly inflating numbers of livestock predation by wolves, in some cases reporting numbers ten times higher than those of the Department of Interior's Fish and Wildlife Service. So skewed are the numbers that as a result, politicians in western states initiated a campaign in 2021 to delist gray wolves from the Endangered Species Act of 1973. A court blocked this effort shortly after, citing lack of scientific evidence. A congressional rider nevertheless allowed for the killing of wolves in Utah, Idaho, Wyoming, and Montana. Wolves are now legally subjected in these states to shooting (sometimes from helicopters), trapping, gassing, and other cruel killing methods. The state of Idaho even offers a bounty of $2,000 per wolf carcass and, in some cases, no license is required to kill them.

Estimated pre-colonial range

Current range

Reintroduced

Colorado is once again at the center of the debate around native predators. In the 2020 election, voters narrowly passed Prop 114, which mandated the reintroduction of wolves on the western slope of the Rocky Mountains inside the state. Hunting organizations vigorously opposed the legislation, claiming that wolves compete with them for valuable game animals like elk, the natural prey of wolves. Similar reintroductions of wolves were successful in Yellowstone National Park in the 1990s, where the ecosystem underwent a drastic, positive change as a result. Because wolves are a keystone species, their removal negatively affects every link in the food chain. Without them, large herbivores explode in population, overgraze native plants, and degrade soil health. Plants die and bird populations vanish. Trees that shade rivers disappear, hurting fish populations, which in turn hurts their predators. The reduction in carcasses left by wolves threatens scavengers, too. It's clear that despite the bloated bottom lines of the livestock industry, wolves are essential to a healthy environment for all of us.

BLACK-BILLED Magpies

Pica hudsonia

Like other corvids, magpies have been the object of superstition since the 18th century. According to some, the sight of a magpie might foretell anything from bad weather to certain death. While some of these legends have faded in the cultural milieu, not much has changed about the magpie's bad rap. Farmers and ranchers blame them for damage to fruit and nut crops as well as livestock deaths, even though they consume a variety of crop pests themselves, and there is little evidence of magpies killing livestock. Magpies actually enjoy a symbiotic relationship with cattle, often seen perching on their backs in search of ticks to eat: a welcome relief for cattle and an easy meal for the magpie. Magpies are also expert builders who fortify their nests with a layer of mud, making them last for years, allowing them to often be utilized by other birds for shelter during the winter. While magpies may not be totally innocent, it's clear that they give more than they take.

While native to North America, the cowbird is one of the most hated birds by backyard birders and ecologists alike. They're famously derided for being obligate brood parasites, as these negligent parents leave their eggs in other birds' nests. Cowbirds rely on other species to feed and raise their young, never building nests of their own. Not only that, but they also destroy the eggs of other birds, contributing to the decline of endangered warblers. Once confined to the plains, brown-headed cowbirds have since expanded their range to encompass almost all of North America. While we lament their effects on other species, once again we can thank ourselves for the cowbird's preeminence since human development and the increase of their desired habitat of open fields and forest edges caused this expansion. While we may want to mistakenly judge their behavior on the axis of human morality, the evolutionary strategy of the cowbird is neither unique nor their fault.

NO

From the Adiron

TH
acks to Alaska

Canada Geese
Branta canadensis
honk
honk
honk
honk

Canada geese, unaffectionately nicknamed "honkers," are prevalent throughout the U.S. and Canada, and have become a regular feature of suburban living. In some areas, it seems as though wherever there is grass, there is a flock of Canada geese. They have been labeled a nuisance and falsely characterized as inherently mean, aggressive animals. While they are known to be territorial with one another and protective of their eggs and young, Canada geese don't attack humans without provocation. They tend to flock to open fields with short vegetation to feed, using nearby bodies of water to escape from predators like coyotes and bobcats. In today's world, they're a common sight in lots of areas designed for human recreation like golf courses, lawns, parks, and fields. Large numbers of them congregate, honk loudly, and leave droppings that can spread diseases and parasites to humans, but as native migratory birds, they are protected by the Migratory Bird Treaty Act. However, they are still legally hunted in regulated seasons and are targets of all manner of abuse by those who perceive them as nothing more than a nuisance species.

While we may perceive Canada geese as pests, it's important to understand why. For starters, humans are to blame for creating the perfect artificial habitat for them. As development increases throughout the continent, grassy lawns become more prevalent while predator populations continue to be pushed out of urban and suburban areas. The loss of natural habitat, combined with the safety and comfort provided by human infrastructure, has even curtailed annual migrations. As temperatures continue to rise, Canada geese even migrate less far south than they used to. All in all, we've created a world to which they've been forced to adapt, so it's only fair that we adapt as well.

BEARS

The American black bear (Ursus americanus) and brown bear (Ursus arctos) are the most common bears in North America.

As opportunistic omnivores, bears will eat almost anything that's available, in some cases, up to 80 pounds (36kg) of food per day. In the wild, they eat grasses, flowers, berries, tubers, fish, and scavenge other predators' kills of elk or deer. With a sense of smell 100 times greater than humans, bears can smell food over a mile (1.6km) away. They can even remember and return to food sources once they've found them. Thus, they break into inadequately secured garbage and feast on campsites, beehives, orchards, and corn crops. Of course, as humans encroach farther into increasingly limited bear habitat, conflicts increase. Extreme weather caused by climate change further limits their access to food, encouraging bears to seek out an easy meal from humans. Because younger bears are the most likely to seek out human food, the best way to control nuisance bears is not to hunt them, but to remove their access to human food sources.

Bears are feared because of their formidable size and strength and are often shot on sight. However, there are only one or two dozen bear attacks each year in all of North America on average; one is about 60,000 times more likely to be killed by another human than a bear. In fact, most of their behavior we find threatening (like bluff charging) is often designed to ward off predators like us, not attack. As ecosystem engineers, bears are crucial to the environment. They are more efficient at seed dispersal than most birds, and bears who eat fish also help fertilize soil with their nitrogen-rich droppings, which even increase biodiversity on forest floors. Like wolves, bears also help to keep large herbivore populations in check. Unfortunately, brown bears are considered threatened in the U.S. due to habitat loss, climate change, and until recently, unregulated hunting.

Muskrats are semiaquatic rodents who live in wetlands. Spending most of their lives in or near water, they can hold their breath under water for over 15 minutes. Despite their small size, they can create problems for humans; man-made water management structures like dams, retaining walls, and levees are damaged or destroyed where erosion caused by burrowing has led to their collapse. Muskrats can wreak havoc on golf courses, too, tunneling through the banks of man-made ponds to evade predators. They are also regularly accused of damaging rice crops and raiding aquaculture facilities for farmed mussels and crayfish. However, muskrats are crucial prey for predators in wetland ecosystems like snapping turtles, herons, and even fish like largemouth bass. Thanks to their appetite for aquatic plant roots, muskrats help maintain healthy populations of cattails and other plants, providing a variety of food for waterfowl and other aquatic animals. Once again, we blame an animal for acting on instinct, getting in the way of our plans to curate a wild environment for our exclusive use, but fail to consider the bigger picture.

Many other species use muskrat lodges after they've been vacated.

Muskrats

Ondatra zibethicus

BEAVERS

Castor canadensis

Beavers are both a keystone species and ecosystem engineers par excellence. Not only does their presence keep other species in balance, but their ability to alter the environment is second only to humans. Sadly, beavers who live near humans are reduced to a mere inconvenience. They down trees in suburban neighborhoods causing road closures and power outages, and their dams can flood roads as well as airport runways. Unfortunately, when beavers are removed from an ecosystem, plant biodiversity fades, wetlands go dry, and all kinds of animals disappear. Climate change only makes the beaver more critical, as their presence in forest habitats often assists in limiting wildfires, and their dams can help to control ever more common flash flooding. Moreover, they slow the flow of water, so that in drought conditions, wetlands stay wet, keeping other animals alive. As pollution increases, beaver dams act as natural filters by absorbing toxic chemicals in the water. All told, beavers benefit us and the planet; they are the superheroes of the natural world.

No matter how beneficial they are, in some states, beavers are still routinely hunted for their pelts, trapped, and killed due to what we consider nuisance behavior. They are also sometimes poisoned by pollutants found in the water where they live. Despite beavers being our potential allies in the fight against the climate crisis, we seem to think only of how their natural behavior inconveniences us.

Porcupines

Erethizon dorsatum

Aka "quill pigs."

Porcupines live in coniferous forests with few natural predators. Dogs overcome with curiosity are the most common accidental victims of the porcupine, failing as they do to heed the hissing and teeth-chattering warning of the porcupine before they receive a nose full of quills. Frequently dining on the bark of pine trees, porcupines alter their growth, rendering the trees unusable for the logging industry, instead making them suitable homes for birds and bats. They have a particular taste for salt, chewing on anything that might have even a trace of it, including tools once held by sweaty human hands and tires salty from winter de-icing. As ecosystem engineers, they should be respected and protected. When porcupines prune trees, fruit and branches fall from the canopy, providing larger, non-climbing animals with crucial nutrients and the forest floor with light, thus promoting biodiversity. The dead wood that porcupines leave helps insect populations, too, which provides food for birds and bears. These unassuming, prickly "pests" have a job to do, and we would do well to let them do it.

WOLVERINES

Gulo gulo

Aka "woods devil," "glutton," or "skunk bear."

They have very wide paws so they can easily traverse snowy terrain in pursuit of prey and shelter.

With the ability to take down animals over ten times their size, wolverines are some of the most fearsome predators in the Arctic. Their teeth and jaws are so strong that they can even consume the teeth of the animals they kill. Unfortunately, they were once considered a nuisance to settlers moving west and were extirpated from most of the contiguous U.S. in the early 20th century due to unregulated fur trapping and hunting. With the removal of bears and wolves from high alpine areas of the Rockies, wolverines were secondary victims, as a large part of their diet relies on scavenging wolf and bear kills. Today, they are illegally shot because they're considered competition by fur trappers. They prey on the fur industry's targets and often take their kills, even burying traps in the snow. With only around 300 wolverines remaining in the lower 48 states of the U.S., they were listed under the Endangered Species Act in 2023. Thankfully, Colorado is moving forward with a plan to reintroduce 30 to 45 wolverines, much to the dismay of the ski tourism industry and purveyors of livestock. As climate change threatens the snow they depend on for shelter, storing food, and raising young, their populations are already at risk. As is the case with so many wild animals, the best thing we can do for them is leave them alone.

Their jaws are adapted to crush bone and their teeth are sharp enough to tear through flesh, so they easily break into canned food when they encounter hunters' stashes.

Elk are scorned by farmers and ecologists alike, because without predators like wolves in many of their natural habitats, they can overgraze while they forage, damaging ecosystems in the process. At a sustainable level, elk are adept at managing plant populations. They graze, migrate, and disperse seeds through their droppings, promoting biodiversity. Elk draw ecotourists from all over the world to national and state parks in the U.S. and Canada. In Estes Park, Colorado, entire herds of elk frequently graze on golf courses, and sometimes even wander through the downtown, wholly unfazed by onlookers who delight in their majestic presence. Like many animals, when elk become habituated to humans, they can sometimes become fearful, irritated, or aggressive, especially during breeding seasons. They can charge people in defense of their calves and mates, as well, so it's always best to admire them from a safe distance. Whether it be climate change, ecotourism, or habitat loss, the blame for the so-called nuisances that elk present once again rest squarely on the shoulders of humans.

MOOSE

Alces alces

Standing at up to seven feet (2m) tall at the shoulder and weighing up to 1,600 pounds (725kg), moose are the largest members of the deer family. Their enormous size and speed (up to 35 miles/56 kilometers per hour) makes them too big for most predators to take on, but the weak and/or sick become critical prey for black bears and wolves. Like elk, moose are known to graze on crops and gardens, but because they are mostly solitary animals, their impact is limited.

Moose often drink water on roadsides containing salt from de-icing.

Moose have notoriously poor eyesight.

Climate change and habitat loss are the main factors threatening moose today, as they depend on young forests in cold climates. However, vehicle collisions with moose are a growing concern as humans encroach on their habitat and ecotourism increases. While their dark pelage helps them retain heat in winter months, it makes it difficult for drivers to see them crossing roads at night. A staggering 3,000 vehicle collisions involving moose occur in North America each year, 800 in Alaska alone. Because of their large size, human fatality or critical injury is high. However, speed is often the determining risk factor, so the least we can do to protect them is slow down.

UBIQ
PE
C

All Over

IOUS

TS

th America

Pigeons

Columba livia

Pigeons were not only a staple at dinner tables, but also reliable messengers and cherished companions across the world for thousands of years before they were brought to North America as game birds. When some of them escaped captivity, populations exploded quickly in areas along the U.S. East Coast. With the rise of technology, their use as messengers fell out of favor, and they were all but abandoned, with the last homing pigeon retiring from the UK military in 1948. As a result, virtually all of the pigeons we see today are not wild birds, but feral descendants of their wild predecessors. Pigeons have since adapted to live near humans in urban environments, with man-made structures becoming their preferred habitats. Human population centers have also made it easier for pigeons to find food, despite what seems to be our collective disdain for them.

Sadly, this cultural shift has made a cartoonish villain of the humble pigeon. In the 1960s, we started to condemn them as "rats with wings," insisting they spread disease, and labeling flocks as infestations. In reality, epidemiologists say pigeons are no danger to humans; if left to their own devices, they pose very little threat. Yet, these docile, defenseless birds are routinely sterilized, kicked, shot, or worse. Despite their current reputation, pigeons are an integral part of human history. They were written about in Mesopotamia, spread the news of Olympic wins in Ancient Greece, and even served in both world wars. We bred pigeons for our own purposes, and now that we no longer need them, we should respect their history by honoring their presence.

Deer

Odocoileus virginianus

white-tailed deer

Our childhoods are filled with fond memories of cartoon woodland creatures like deer, yet for most adults, deer are an unwelcome sight. Some see them as not merely an inconvenience, but a destructive force that must be lethally removed. Ironically, we have created the perfect habitat for them to flourish and proliferate. Deforestation across the continent for agricultural and residential use has provided deer with the forest edges adjacent to open, grassy clearings they prefer. Today, despite being hunted to near extirpation in the 1800s, deer are the most abundant large mammals in North America.

Deer are often hated by farmers because of their fondness for soybeans and corn. They also frustrate orchard owners for eating their fruit, and are particularly vexing to gardeners as they decapitate carefully planted flowers and vegetables. Unfortunately, deer are known to aid in the spread of Lyme disease because of the ticks that plague them. Sadly, they're also blamed for more than one million car collisions in North America each year. Ecologists and civilians agree that overpopulation seems to be at the root of deer problems. Like elk, when deer are at a sustainable population, they benefit the ecosystem. When predators are removed and their preferred habitat increases, all bets are off. The good news is that human desire and ingenuity have provided solutions that benefit deer, the ecosystem, and ourselves. Experimental but controversial sterilization efforts have proven to be more effective than hunting. One such program at the National Institute of Health campus in Maryland reduced the deer population by 47 percent over just three years. Despite their efficacy, sterilization campaigns are unpopular with wildlife managers due to the cost associated with their implementation. Highway overpasses specifically designed for wildlife have proven to reduce 97 percent of collisions involving wild animals. Today, there are over a thousand such structures in the U.S., with more on the way in Colorado and Arizona. Despite expensive construction, wildlife overpasses are cost-effective, too, according to a Washington State University study. Wildlife-related collisions result in an estimated $8 billion in property damage annually, to say nothing of medical costs associated with injuries, and taxpayer dollars spent on emergency services and carcass removal. Whether we like it or not, deer are our neighbors, not invaders, and like any good neighbor, we can implement fair solutions to resolve our squabbles with them.

Mallards

Wherever there are slow-moving waters or ponds, there are probably mallards. The signature green heads of males are synonymous with ducks in western culture. Mallards are the common ancestor of nearly all domestic ducks, often hybridizing with feral populations. They are unwelcome guests at golf courses, pools, and parks, where they are accused of spreading disease, contaminating water, and generally being in the way. While some hate them, others delight in their presence. Many well-intentioned people contribute to the mallard's nuisance status and poor health, however, when they feed them bread and other snacks designed for humans. Not only does bread lack nutritional value for ducks; it expands in their stomachs, giving them an artificial feeling of satiation. Calcium deficiency caused by lack of proper nutrition can also cause conditions like metabolic bone disease in ducks, in which bone malformations can render them flightless and thus more dependent on people. Leftover bread not only attracts unwanted scavengers, but also aspergillus, a fungus that can cause fatal lung conditions in waterfowl. Moreover, as mallards become accustomed to being fed, they return to easy food sources, which can lead to overcrowding and competition among sparring ducks, resulting in injuries. Like many animals who depend on water for food and shelter, mallards are often poisoned by pollution, too, especially by oil in stormwater runoff.

Despite interference from humans, mallards are among the most abundant waterfowl in the world, and their high populations contribute to their positive effects on the ecosystem. Many animals are known for seed dispersal, but mallards are particularly efficient at it. Large flocks move between water sources, foraging a variety of roots, tubers, seeds, and plants, eventually ending up in their home roost. Their droppings are full of diverse plants, which eventually take root and create biodiverse wetland habitats. That said, while many of us mean well, mallards can only help the environment if they are left to their own devices.

Mice

Mus musculus

Mice are unwelcome houseguests to most, largely due to their ability to transmit diseases like salmonellosis, hantavirus, leptospirosis, and choriomeningitis through contact with their droppings or bites. However, mice have lived among us even before the advent of agriculture. Feeding on stored or growing grains (their favorite food), mice have expanded their populations alongside humanity. Like any other mammal, including us, mice seek warmth and shelter during winter months, often finding themselves inside houses, cars, and barns. Their habit of gnawing can even cause electrical fires and damage household appliances. These critters don't eat much, but they contaminate large amounts of food meant for humans.

The human imagination has conjured regrettably cruel methods to exterminate mice, most of which secondarily harm other animals, too. Labels on rodenticides often warn users of potential harm it can do to their pets and children, yet people readily deploy powerful poisons on unwitting mice—the result of which is typically slow, internal bleeding that eventually leads to their deaths. Predators like owls who eat mice can then become secondarily poisoned. Glue traps leave mice to slowly die of suffocation, starvation, dehydration, or exhaustion, and inadvertently relegate birds and snakes to the same sticky, torturous death. Humane traps require more effort and vigilance but are better for the planet and less dangerous for humans as well as our pets. Exclusion is the best way to ensure our homes are free of mice; pest control companies often offer mouse-proofing as a service, sealing all possible entrances. Because they are not protected by the Animal Welfare Act, over 100 million mice and rats are subjected to unregulated cruelty and euthanasia in research laboratories, often in vain because 95 percent of drugs tested on animals fail during human trials. While it's understandable not to want mice living among us, cruelty is not only unnecessary: It doesn't work, either.

Rats

Rattus norvegicus

"Rat" has become a moniker in the West for an untrustworthy, corrupt thief, even though the truth about rats is that they are a smart, social, and resourceful species just trying to survive. The long-held belief that the Black Death was caused by fleas attached to black rats has been debunked. Due to the speed of its transmission, scientists now believe it was humans carrying lice and fleas who spread the disease. That the humble rat was blamed for the Black Death plague for centuries when, in fact, the culprit was us, is sadly common; like so many animals, we hold them responsible for problems we create, however inadvertently. Rats do carry disease and cause billions of dollars in property damage each year, but they're only able to do this because we provide them with endless supplies of food in the form of garbage, and shelter in the form of crumbling infrastructure in which they can easily find homes.

Because rats can eat almost anything, human refuse is enough to sustain them. City-wide trapping and killing efforts have proven to be far less effective than employing smarter waste management practices. No matter what governments do, as long as people litter, there will be rats. Additionally, climate change is providing rats with longer warm seasons and shorter, milder winters, allowing them to survive and breed longer. Despite their reputation for being dirty, rats are cleaner than most dogs; much like cats, they spend a great deal of their lives bathing, and they keep very tidy nests with separate areas for sleeping, storing food, and excrement. When kept as pets, rats are known to bond with humans, though as social animals, they shouldn't be kept without another rat. One experiment even showed that they will choose to rescue each other from traps over a food source. Rats are also among the most intelligent mammals, as they have outperformed humans in some cognitive tests and can easily solve complex puzzles. They can even be trained to detect tuberculosis in humans, saving lives. Rats may not be cuddly or cute to some, but we certainly should be kinder to them.

Cottontail Rabbits

Cottontails are among the most abundant and heavily preyed upon mammals in North America, crucial for the diets of foxes, bobcats, owls, hawks, and others. Unfortunately, the cottontail population (comprised of multiple species) has faced a sharp decline over the past 50 years, mostly due to land development for agricultural use. That hasn't stopped the cottontail from being viewed as a simple garden pest, though. During warmer months, they are notorious for making buffets out of residential vegetable and flower gardens; they particularly enjoy leafy greens, cabbage, beets, peas, beans, carrots, young tulips, and roses. Cottontails are also considered agricultural pests because of their fondness of berries. In winter, they rely on tree buds and small branches of young dogwood, sugar maple, and apple trees as well as ornamental shrubs, frustrating landowners and purveyors of commercial forests.

Cottontails are voracious herbivores, and not picky eaters; studies show they eat 145 different plant species, helping to maintain diverse meadow ecosystems in the wild. Luckily for us, they love to eat weeds, including dandelions. Unfortunately, the use of herbicides containing the carcinogenic chemical glyphosate is widespread throughout the world, so much so that studies on human urine found residue of the chemical in the vast majority of participants. In 2020, the U.S. Environmental Protection Agency also found that the use of glyphosate can kill or injure up to 93 percent of all endangered species. That being said, when welcomed into our lawns and gardens, wild rabbits like the cottontail could be viewed as an alternative, natural herbicide. Their presence could reduce the impact our lawns have on our health and the environment, all while also saving us from the tedium that is digging out weeds with a trowel.

HOUSE SPARROWS

Passer domesticus

For better or worse, most species' survival is inextricably tied to human behavior. Fortunately for the house sparrow, we have all but ensured their dominance throughout the world. Originally native to Eurasia and Africa, house sparrows were intentionally released in Brooklyn, New York to help combat growing insect populations in 1851. Following their success, other American cities implemented similar protocols. Today, house sparrows are in every U.S. state, but they are unable to survive in many natural environments and can only live around humans. They possess adaptive genes dating back to the birth of agriculture some 10,000 years ago, when they evolved to eat starchy grains and common agricultural crops, and developed stronger beaks to crack seeds sown by humans.

Unfortunately, they compete with native birds for food and shelter and are often aggressive and territorial toward their avian brethren. While it's easy to resent them, we must again look to ourselves when assigning responsibility: while unintentional, these are the consequences of trading one inconvenience for another. Whether we like it or not, with a population of 7 million in the U.S. alone, these scrappy, dust-bathing birds are here to stay.

BARN SWALLOWS

Hirundo rustica

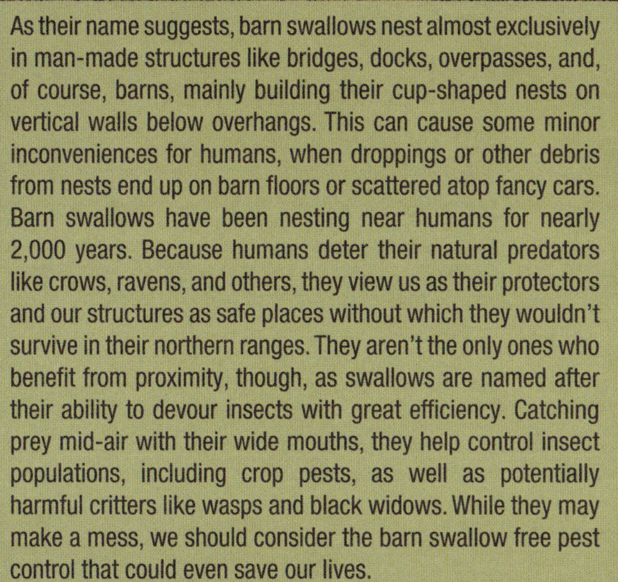

As their name suggests, barn swallows nest almost exclusively in man-made structures like bridges, docks, overpasses, and, of course, barns, mainly building their cup-shaped nests on vertical walls below overhangs. This can cause some minor inconveniences for humans, when droppings or other debris from nests end up on barn floors or scattered atop fancy cars. Barn swallows have been nesting near humans for nearly 2,000 years. Because humans deter their natural predators like crows, ravens, and others, they view us as their protectors and our structures as safe places without which they wouldn't survive in their northern ranges. They aren't the only ones who benefit from proximity, though, as swallows are named after their ability to devour insects with great efficiency. Catching prey mid-air with their wide mouths, they help control insect populations, including crop pests, as well as potentially harmful critters like wasps and black widows. While they may make a mess, we should consider the barn swallow free pest control that could even save our lives.

Barn swallows catch their prey in flight rather than foraging on the ground like house sparrows.

Barn swallows build their nests by mixing mud and grass, which can take up to 5 days.

house sparrows

female

male

RACCOONS

Procyon lotor

Affectionately called "nature's bandits" due to their quintessential black facemask, raccoons are known to break into trash cans, take up residence in chimneys, steal chicken eggs, harass household pets, raid gardens, and orchestrate a number of other illicit activities deemed bothersome to humans. Native to North America, raccoons prefer woodlands but have adapted to live near us thanks to the easy access to food and shelter that we provide. Proximity costs them, too, however; in addition to being disdained for their sometimes destructive behavior, raccoons are often feared as spreaders of disease. But since they're most active at night, it's easy for humans to avoid direct contact with them, mitigating the risk of diseases like rabies and parvovirus. Raccoons also tend to wash their food before consuming it: another plot hole in the dirty narrative we've assigned to them.

The common English name for raccoons derives from the Algonquian name *arakun,* which roughly translates to "he who scratches with his hands." They may be infamous for the nimble little paws that make them adept at thievery and purveyors of mischief, but raccoons also serve as nature's cleaning crew. Their opportunistic diet includes carrion, which helps prevent the spread of disease due to the potentially harmful bacteria and parasites present in the decaying flesh. Like many animals, raccoons also promote biodiversity by spreading the seeds of plants in their droppings. They may raid our perfectly manicured gardens and landscaping, but they're helping maintain ecosystems and protecting the environment, too.

Crows + Ravens

As some of the most intelligent birds on the planet, crows and ravens can outperform human children in problem-solving tests. Smart and scrappy, these birds can have an attitude, too; they can mimic human speech, remember human faces, and hold grudges. Crows can even warn their families of humans they don't like and, as they defend their territories, may subject people to a behavior known as "mobbing," where groups of crows squawk at and harass the offending human. Crows and ravens can also plan for the future, an ability once thought to be exclusive to humans and apes. Despite their intelligence, crows are perceived by many of us as mere squawking garbage eaters. As opportunistic omnivores, they're seen devouring anything from roadkill to someone's stolen doughnut. They often eat pet food, break into trash, and raid gardens for fruits and nuts. As urbanization has increased, so have crow populations in cities. Cities and suburbs provide ample food sources, light pollution that protects them from nocturnal predators, and the heat-island effect, all of which make these locales more attractive to crows.

Crows and ravens are also among the most culturally symbolic birds in the world. Often invoked as omens of death, war, and evil, crows and ravens have been unfairly persecuted. Groups of crows are famously called "murders," and while mostly solitary animals, when ravens do congregate, it is referred to as an "unkindness." Famed gothic poet Edgar Allen Poe's poem, "The Raven," used the bird to symbolize grief and death; today, the Baltimore Ravens owe their NFL team name to this iconic poem. In the Bible, ravens have been interpreted as a symbol of vice. Odin, the Norse and Pagan god of war, was often pictured flanked by two ravens named Huginn and Muninn, translating to "memory" and "wisdom," respectively. However, many indigenous peoples of North America exalt the crow as both the creator and a trickster god. Clearly, crows and ravens are iconic, relatable pillars of human culture. All in all, these mischievous, intelligent birds are a lot like us: complicated, protective, and a little mean, but just trying to survive.

Chipmunks are small, mouse-sized rodents related to prairie dogs, and are similarly known for burrowing. With just a two-inch diameter opening, their burrows are usually three feet (1m) deep and 30 feet (9m) long, holding multiple chambers where they store caches of food for the winter. When living near humans, chipmunks tend to dig burrows near flower beds, patios, retention walls, and woodpiles. Because they cover up the original hole used to dig the burrow and carry dirt in their cheek pouches, their burrows are usually inconspicuous and don't cause structural damage to property. Unfortunately for gardeners, chipmunks are particularly fond of vegetables, flowers, and bulbs, but they also eat berries, larvae, slugs, and other invertebrates, too.

Chipmunks

Chipmunks are famous for their specialized cheek pouches that, much like Mary Poppins's carpet bag, have a seemingly infinite capacity. In fact, research shows they can hold as many as 12 acorns at a time—impressive considering their diminutive stature. As seed dispersers, they help increase biodiversity in their woodland habitats. Chipmunks also eat mushrooms, which benefits tree growth when they release spores that help tree roots absorb nutrients through the mycorrhizal network, a symbiotic nutrient exchange highway between trees and fungi.

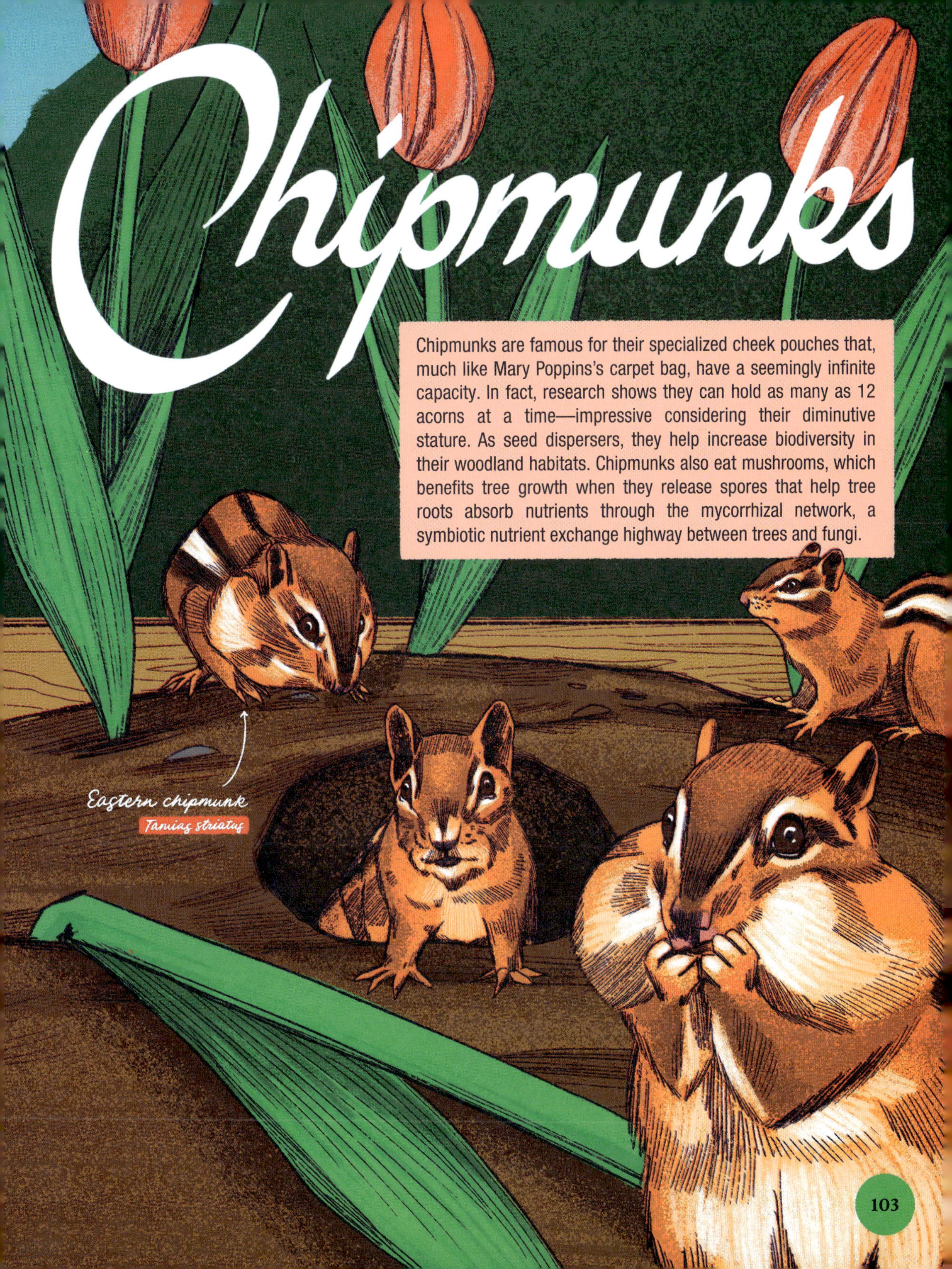

Seagulls

"Seagulls" are not a single type of bird, but rather a colloquial term for many birds with similar characteristics. Moreover, not all gulls live near the coast. Nearly everyone who's ever visited a beach has witnessed menacing flocks of gulls swooping from the sky in hot pursuit of boardwalk fries, seemingly flaunting the spoils of victory around crying, newly fry-less children. While we may see them as a blight on our otherwise relaxing beach vacations, the feeling is apparently mutual. Research shows that herring gulls dislike people, and they go to great lengths to avoid being looked at by us.

In addition to their bad beach etiquette, they are a major headache to the aviation industry; gulls are the victims in nearly one third of bird-related aircraft incidents. In addition, their tendency to flock to landfills in search of food even causes accidents involving heavy equipment and trucks at waste management facilities. Despite the chaos they sow, gulls do serve as critical beach cleanup crews and pest control operations. They eat washed-up seaweed and dead fish on the shore along with other carrion, and in urban areas, they're known to eat rats. Herring gulls can be helpful to fishermen, often leading them to schools of fish.

Woodpeckers

Woodpeckers all over the world vary in size, color, diet, and habitat, but they all have one thing in common: as their name suggests, they peck cavities in trees. Woodpeckers depend on trees for food and shelter, so they tend to live in or near forests or heavily wooded suburban areas. They usually get their food by creating small holes in standing dead trees called snags, using their long, sticky, barbed tongues to gather insects from the decaying wood. People are often exasperated by their habit of hammering away at wooden siding; like little avian jackhammers, they poke unsightly holes and make a great deal of noise. If one's house is a frequent buffet for woodpeckers, they can thank woodpeckers for detecting a possible insect infestation early on. Woodpeckers don't just make noise as a consequence of foraging or nesting, though; they use the noise to establish their territories and to attract mates—a behavior called drumming. Woodpeckers are known to drum on houses, telephone poles, and even road signs because these objects generate more noise than snags.

Woodpeckers are not just resourceful; they're ecosystem engineers and keystone species. Because woodpeckers vary so much in size, their abandoned nesting cavities are depended on by hundreds of other animals around the world. In fact, woodpeckers create 90 percent of tree cavities, with the remaining occurring naturally. Without woodpeckers, secondary cavity nesters like owls, squirrels, songbirds, and swallows would have far fewer places to nest and hide from predators. The famously large pileated woodpecker has seamlessly taken up the ecological niche of the near-extinct ivory-billed woodpecker, whose abandoned nest cavities are large enough to support wood ducks and barred owls. As true stewards of the forest, woodpeckers help the cycle of growth and decay, too; researchers recently discovered that some woodpeckers are carriers of wood-eating fungi, which accelerates the decay of dead wood, providing food for insects and other birds, as well as room for new growth. Considering their role in the ecosystem, we might be inclined to forgive the noise and destruction woodpeckers may inadvertently cause.

For hundreds of years, foxes have been anthropomorphized as fraudulent, cunning infiltrators in an array of religions, media, and pop culture. The Catholic Church's bestiary depicted the fox as the symbol of the devil, which led to the burning of foxes in the Middle Ages. Some etymologists say the word "shenanigan" originates from the Gaelic *sionnachuighim,* or "I play the fox." Today, foxes are still haunted by their reputation as thieving antagonists, as common idioms like "don't let a fox guard the henhouse" are baked into the cake of today's culture. While most people don't take such metaphors literally, our collective feelings toward foxes have real-life consequences. They are unfairly persecuted, partially because we assign human morals to their natural instincts and punish them accordingly.

FOXES

Vulpes vulpes

The fox affectionately dubbed the "Capitol Fox," who became famous among Washington, D.C., locals for prowling the grounds of the U.S. Congress, even garnered a following on ghost-written social media accounts. The rabies-infected fox and her three kits were euthanized in 2022 after a dust-up with a sitting congressman while protecting her den. It's true that foxes are adept predators, but most of the time their instincts benefit us. Not only do they control rodent populations, but they also keep other predators in check because they compete with them for prey. In fact, farmers have been known to reintroduce foxes to areas where crop-eating rodents have become hard to manage. While most see the fox as solely a predator, they are fond of berries and other fruits, too, which makes them great seed dispersers that help ecosystems thrive.

Weasels

In northern populations, weasels like the stoat, least weasel, and long-tailed weasel grow white winter coats in order to camouflage themselves in the snow to hide from predators.

Like foxes, weasels are the victims of cultural smear campaigns. Common phrases like "weasel words," and "weaseling out," are used to describe stealthy, corrupt swindlers who evade accountability. While we tend to anthropomorphize and hyperbolize weasels' behavior, there are some truths to these stereotypes; despite their size, weasels are impressively lethal predators. They are known for killing more prey than they could possibly devour and storing caches of kills in burrows. One weasel burrow was even found containing the carcasses of over 150 voles. While it may seem gluttonous to us, weasels' prey drive is not triggered by hunger, but rather detection of movement. Though weasels vastly prefer a diet of wild rodents (whose populations they help control), this behavior unfortunately extends to chicken coops, as they can "weasel" into openings one inch or larger. Despite their propensity for seemingly indiscriminate killing, it is simply a result of natural instinct for which they shouldn't be punished.

Long-tailed weasel
Neogale frenata

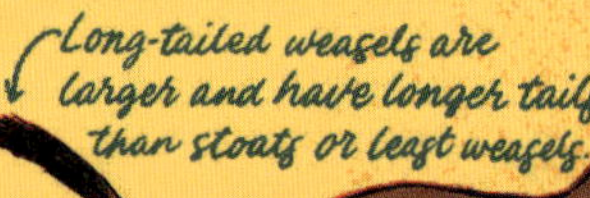

Long-tailed weasels are larger and have longer tails than stoats or least weasels.

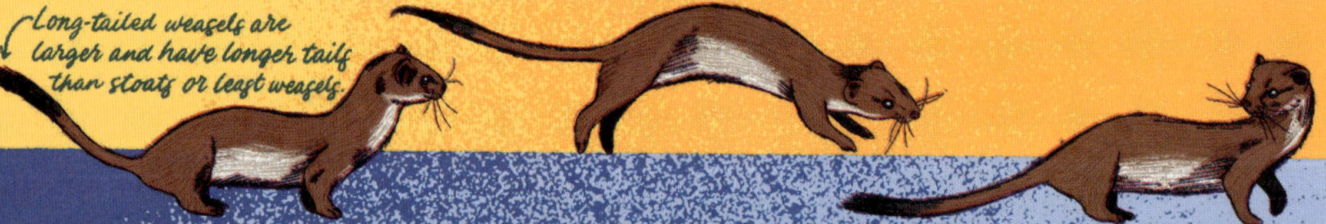

BOBCATS

Lynx rufus

While bobcats are elusive, crepuscular felids that are rarely seen by humans, we still blame them for plenty of problems. Much like our pet cats, bobcats are known to carry diseases like cat scratch fever and toxoplasmosis, though without direct contact with bobcats (or their feces) risk of transmission is entirely avoidable. They are also blamed for the deaths of sheep, chickens, and the occasional calf, but statistics show that bobcat depredation is exceedingly rare, and is often a case of mistaken identity. Bobcats do, however, occasionally break into residential chicken coops, garbage, and outdoor pet food caches that haven't been properly secured. While bobcats are opportunistic predators who are able to diversify their diet in the absence of their natural prey, they mostly eat rodents and rabbits, and help to control their populations. However, the use of rodenticide has had grave effects on bobcats. Adult bobcats are too large for the dose found in rodents to kill them, but repeated exposure to anticoagulants have long-term effects on their immune systems, which correlate with a rise in notoedric mange (scabies) in bobcats. If we just left bobcats to their own devices and did our part to protect them, bobcats could make for much better neighbors.

Starlings

Sturnus vulgaris

Rumors abound regarding how European starlings were intentionally introduced to North America in the 19th century. Whether they were originally introduced to combat insect populations in New York City or by a Shakespeare fanatic obsessed with the birds the famed playwright wrote about, European starlings are now among the most abundant invasive birds on the continent. Eating livestock feed, nesting in exhaust fans, and causing millions of dollars in cleanup and fruit crop damage every year, starlings endure a poor reputation. However, some say their ecological impact is overblown. Research shows there is little correlation between the decline in native birds and the presence of starlings, as some native birds have even adapted their behavior to accommodate the presence of starlings. Habitat loss and climate change have certainly increased competition between starlings and native birds, but starlings didn't arrive here unabetted. Once again, we must hold ourselves responsible for their proliferation.

RED-WINGED BLACKBIRDS

Male red-winged blackbirds are easily recognized by their red and yellow shoulder patches (called epaulets). Known for roosting in large numbers and flocking in murmurations with other birds like starlings and grackles, red-winged blackbirds are similarly hated by purveyors of corn and sunflower crops. They feed on immature crops, and though they are protected by the Migratory Bird Treaty Act, red-winged blackbirds are illegally poisoned and shot to protect agricultural production. They are also labeled aggressive because of their tendency to dive-bomb people, animals, and other birds in defense of their territories. Despite their reputation, red-winged blackbirds help control weeds as well as populations of beetles and weevils, which are known crop pests.

DOMESTIC CATS

Felis catus

While cats may be among the most popular furry companions, when abandoned or otherwise free-ranging, they can be extremely destructive to the environment. Furthermore, feral cats are subject to high mortality associated with exposure, disease, and, of course, human cruelty. Studies show that cats are the primary cause of death to native birds, killing around 2.4 billion worldwide each year. Just one outdoor cat can kill 100 animals annually, including native mammals, reptiles, and amphibians. While some justify feral and outdoor cat populations as free pest control, studies show that cats do not significantly affect invasive rodent populations like the house mouse or brown rat; rather, they are more likely to prey on native rodents, causing further harm to ecosystems.

Trap-Neuter-Return (TNR) programs set out to better the health and safety of feral cats. They sterilize, vaccinate, and either return them to where they were found, or bring them to adoption centers if they are socialized to humans. This is said to reduce "yowling" and territorial marking behaviors associated with breeding, which often instigate abuse of feral cats by humans, as well as reduce their risk of euthanasia. While these programs are among the best things we can do for these cats, they do little to curb their ecological impact because they are ineffective at reducing their populations. An astounding 70 percent of feral cats would have to be sterilized for that to happen, an impossible feat considering there are up to 80 million of them in the U.S. alone. Sadly, the only feasible way to reduce outdoor cat populations is to better educate people about responsible pet ownership and seek to further increase pet adoptions.

Squirrels

With a proclivity for darting into oncoming traffic, raiding bird feeders, nesting in attics, and gnawing at the faces of jack-o-lanterns, squirrels are polarizing mainstays of life in North America. While some find squirrels and their antics cute, others see them as vermin, perhaps due to their sheer abundance and success as synanthropes (animals that have successfully adapted to living around humans). Squirrels are so numerous that they can cause up to 50 percent of the power outages that involve wildlife in any given year—they've even shut down the NASDAQ twice: once in 1987 and again in 1994. Sometimes, this can be related to their need to chew on things; like most rodents, their incisors never stop growing, and they need to gnaw on hard surfaces to wear them down so they don't grow into their skulls and injure them. Their teeth can grow up to six inches (15cm) a year!

While some people find them irritating, squirrels are smarter than we might think. Known for their seed-heavy diets, squirrels can cache up to 3,000 seeds each season in preparation for winter, burying them in various locations throughout their territory. Even more impressive, they can relocate these seeds through a combination of scent tracking and memory. They are even known to rebury caches and fake seed burials to fool competing squirrels and other onlookers. Squirrels are among the top seed dispersers, too, as their forgotten caches of seeds often take root, eventually growing into trees and other plants.

Turkey Vultures

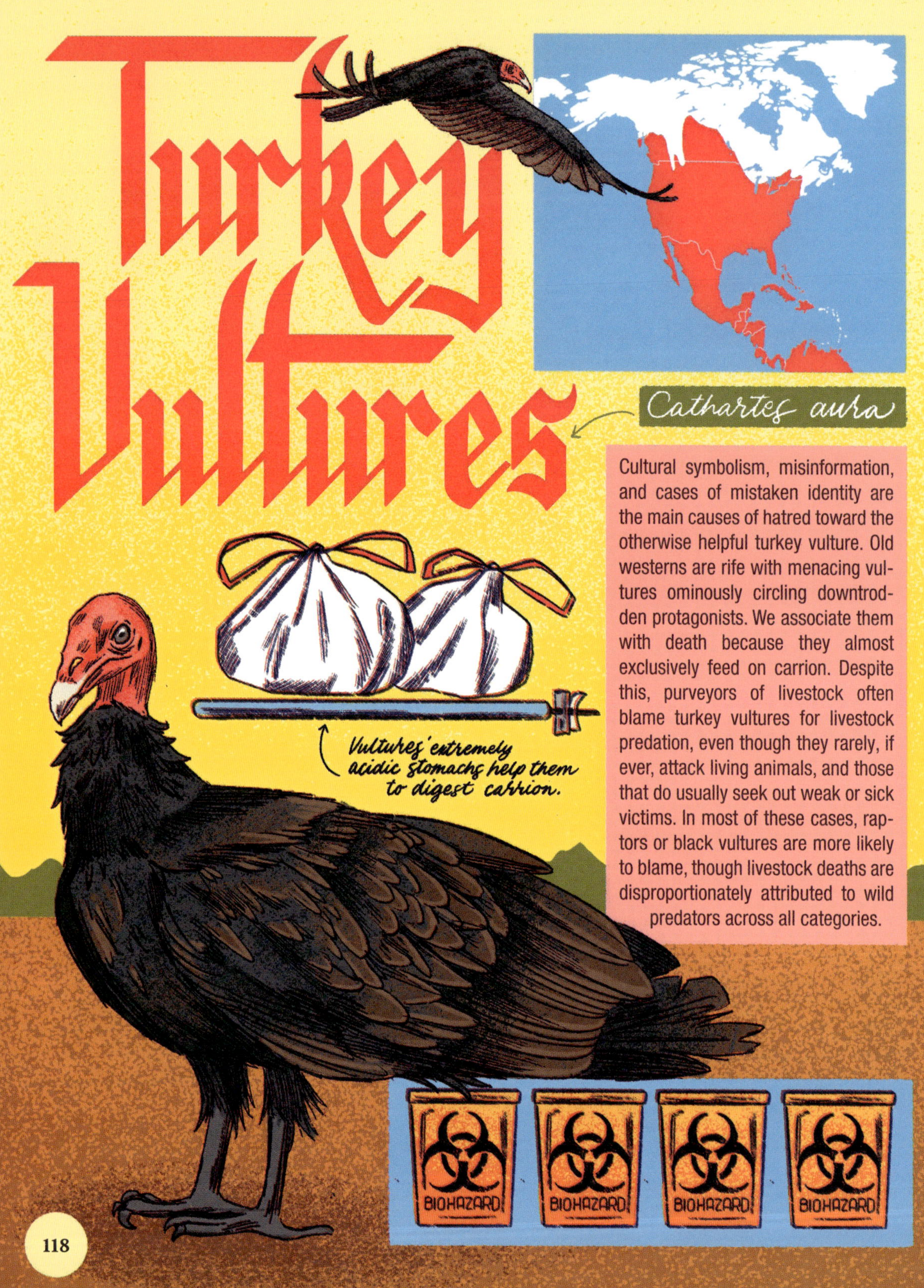

Cultural symbolism, misinformation, and cases of mistaken identity are the main causes of hatred toward the otherwise helpful turkey vulture. Old westerns are rife with menacing vultures ominously circling downtrodden protagonists. We associate them with death because they almost exclusively feed on carrion. Despite this, purveyors of livestock often blame turkey vultures for livestock predation, even though they rarely, if ever, attack living animals, and those that do usually seek out weak or sick victims. In most of these cases, raptors or black vultures are more likely to blame, though livestock deaths are disproportionately attributed to wild predators across all categories.

While their bald heads, hooked beaks, and large wingspans may make them seem intimidating, turkey vultures are gentle birds who do a great service to the environment. Their scientific name, "*Cathartes aura,*" even translates to "cleansing breeze." Their potent stomach acid makes them impervious to diseases like tuberculosis, anthrax, rabies, and distemper when eating infected carcasses. They are among the only birds who use their acute sense of smell to detect food sources; turkey vultures can detect the presence of carrion from over a mile (1.6km) away, making them some of the most effective scavengers in North America. Without turkey vultures, disease could run rampant through animal populations across ecosystems and potentially make their way to us.

SKUNKS

Mephitis mephitis

Skunks are misunderstood as noxious, aggressive terrors, yet are relatively innocuous, if not helpful, critters—especially for gardeners. As solitary and largely nocturnal animals, skunks are easily avoided. Dogs, however, can end up on the wrong end of skirmishes with skunks, so to speak. Curious and clueless to their warnings of stomping, hissing, and charging, dogs can be the victims of skunks' notorious defensive spray. Skunks secrete a sulfur-based liquid from their two anal glands, which when sprayed in a fine mist (up to 20 feet/6 meters away), is an effective eye irritant; it contains chemicals called thiols, which are the same as those found in onions that make us cry. Popular myths tell us to combat the smell of skunk spray by bathing ourselves (or our pets) in tomato juice, but this only serves to mask the scent. Olfactory fatigue caused by the strong aroma of tomatoes causes temporary nose blindness, so the skunk smell will persist unless proper deodorizing methods are implemented.

Skunks can occasionally eat garden tomatoes or other nightshades in our gardens. Usually, however, in the spring and summer they prefer a largely insectivorous diet consisting of grubs, grasshoppers, crickets, larvae, and worms, many of which are garden pests. In fact, when we water our lawns, skunks are attracted to the insects and worms that subsequently emerge, and they may dig small holes in the grass or pull back newly sodded lawns in search of their prey. Because skunks are mostly nomadic, when they den under porches or in other animals' burrows, it's usually only for a few nights—they'll almost certainly move on.

SOURCES

Alabama Wildlife Federation
American Bird Conservancy
Arizona Game & Fish Department
BBC News
California Department of Fish and Wildlife
Cornell Lab of Ornithology
Encyclopedia Britannica
Florida Fish and Wildlife Conservation Commission
Humane World for Animals
Illinois Department of Natural Resources
Indiana Department of Natural Resources
International Union for the Conservation of Nature
Iowa Department of Natural Resources
Loudon Wildlife Conservancy
Maryland Department of Natural Resources
National Audubon Society
National Fish & Wildlife Service
National Park Service
National Public Radio
National Resource Defense Council
National Wildlife Federation
New Mexico Department of Game and Fish
New Mexico Department of Health
North Carolina Wildlife Resource Commission
Ohio Department of Natural Resources
Oregon Public Broadcasting
Parks Canada
Penn State College of Health and Human Development
Public Broadcasting Service
Smithsonian National Zoo and Conservation Biology Institute
SUNY College of Environmental Studies and Forestry
Tennessee Wildlife Resources Agency
Texas Parks and Wildlife Department
United States Department of Agriculture
United States Environmental Protection Agency
United States Forest Service
United States Geological Survey
University of California Integrated Pest Management Program
University of Michigan Department of Zoology
University of Wisconsin–Madison Board of Regents
University of Wisconsin School of Veterinary Medicine
Vermont Fish and Wildlife Department
Virginia Department of Wildlife Resources
Washington Department of Fish & Wildlife
World Wildlife Fund

FOR A FULL BIBLIOGRAPHY, SCAN THE QR CODE:

ACKNOWLEDGMENTS

To my wife, Laurence, who kept me (mostly) sane and picked up the slack while I poured myself into this book. You've been the sounding board for some of my wackiest ideas throughout my career, and have always been a great listener. You were so patient with me when all I could talk about was obscure animal facts, statistics, and the history of pigeons, and let me read my clumsy first drafts aloud when all you wanted to do was unwind after a long day of work. I wouldn't be able to have this career if it wasn't for your generosity, support, and steadiness. I will always be grateful to you. Your rational scientist brain calms my chaotic artist brain; you are truly a balm for my soul.

To my mom, who has always inspired me. Thank you for your unwavering confidence in my dream of being an artist. I will never forget drawing still lifes with you before I hit double digits. You've been my biggest fan since I could hold a pencil, and my teacher long before and after school. You're so often my moral true north; I so admire your passion and respect for all animals, and I can only hope to be half the advocate you are for them. Thank you for raising me, Lily, and Avery to have passion for the world around us, and to create more than we consume. I am an artist because of you, and, as I'm sure they would agree, it is a privilege to be your kid.

To my editor, Alexander Rigby, who plucked me out of obscurity and believed in this book from day one. It has been such a privilege to write and illustrate a book that represents my values and interests so specifically, and I can't thank you enough for letting me make a book about some of the most hated creatures on the planet. You made my first book an incredibly rewarding experience, and I'm so grateful for your patience, guidance, trust, and expertise. Having been an avid reader of DK books since childhood, becoming an author with DK has been the thrill and honor of a lifetime. As I write this, I still can't believe it.

To Casey Smith, who helped me fuse my love of words and drawing, You helped me realize I don't have to choose between them, and I wouldn't be the artist I am today without you.

And lastly, to the reader. If you picked up this book, it means you have empathy in a world that conditions us so relentlessly to lose it. As the world continues to malign and marginalize animals and humans alike, empathy is the only thing that will save us.

INDEX

H

I–J

L

M

N

ABOUT THE AUTHOR

Halsey Berryman (she/her) is an illustrator and lettering artist from Washington, DC, who grew up between DC, Harvard, Massachusetts, and Taos, New Mexico. Halsey received her Bachelor of Fine Arts in 2014 from the Corcoran College of Art + Design, where she studied painting and drawing. While attending art school, she painted signs for grocery stores, which helped launch her multi-pronged freelancing career shortly after. Some of her clients include the Washington Post, AOC for Congress, Sleater-Kinney, Austin City Limits Music Festival, PBS, Bird Collective, and the National Day Laborer Organizing Network. Halsey was featured by the Phillips Collection as part of their Phillips-100 centennial celebration, and was an artist in residence at Fort Lewis College in Durango, Colorado.

Halsey's work explores the interaction between the human and natural world, and what these often humorous exchanges and commonalities can teach us during the Anthropocene. Drawn to the most maligned creatures, Halsey's work is often centered around the underdogs of the animal world, underscoring social and political parallels with animal behavior and cultural signifiers through visual satire. As a dedicated realist, she is inspired by vintage nature illustrations, but as a fan of color, her north star is Risograph printing. Halsey lives in Takoma Park, Maryland with her wife, two dogs, three cats, and a collection of plants.